WHY NOT ADMIT RED CHINA

TO THE

UNITED NATIONS?

by

C. V. Reynolds, Jr.

McCutchan Publishing Corporation
2526 Grove Street
Berkeley, California 94704

ISBN: 0-8211-1712-2
Library of Congress Catalog Card Number: 70-137098

FOREWORD

For over twenty years the policy of the United States has been to isolate mainland China. To isolate a land of that size with a population that comprises approximately one-quarter of the world's population is both difficult and dangerous. Chinese communist missiles will not be stopped by barriers of non-recognition and isolation. Long range problems of human relationships over and above ideological differences will not be solved by non-communication.

The greatest hurdle facing our country is not a generation gap or a credibility gap; it is a knowledge gap. That gap has led to the distressing state of our present involvement in Indochina. We know little about many areas of the world and depressingly little about Asia. Only a few short years ago we had less than a handful of colleges and universities with area studies of Asian nations in their curriculums. Even now we have only a beginning in terms of young men and women with the potential expertise and wisdom to make intelligent decisions in our dealings with those countries.

This book is a valuable contribution to the long-delayed direction of United States academic interest toward the Far East. Toynbee has said that the next watershed of history will be in Asia. We will not serve the interests of our nation or of the world if we continue to wear blinders to avert our eyes and minds from China.

Steps leading to our diplomatic recognition of Communist China and its admission to the United Nations do not constitute moral approval of that government anymore than similar action on our part constituted approval of the policies of the Soviet Union. Further delay will only heighten the degree of distrust between our two nations. The long hard work of negotiations must begin.

Read then, this excellent presentation of our relations with China in the recent past and the arguments why our policies toward China must change. It is a step toward closing our knowledge gap.

HUBERT H. HUMPHREY

CONTENTS

AUTHOR'S PREFACE

During the Korean War, I served aboard a Destroyer Escort as Gunnery Officer. Perhaps because of this close association with the tools of warfare, I became more and more concerned with the horrors of thermonuclear war. After discharge from the naval service, I was an active partner in a construction firm doing work at the Fore River Yard of the Bethlehem Steel Co., Quincy, Massachusetts. Some of our work was done in connection with the construction of the ways for the nuclear-powered cruiser, *USS Long Beach*. My mind became more and more concerned with the dangers resulting from nuclear energy than with admiration for nuclear propulsion.

The major problem in the fifties seemed to be not only lack of nuclear control, but an unwillingness of the world powers to work at effective control and specifically toward a nonproliferation treaty. Fortunately, during the sixties, steps were taken to lessen the delicate balance of terror. Unfortunately, the People's Republic of China has not joined the powers seeking world nuclear control. It is quite certain that Red China will never sign any nonproliferation treaty until it is a member of the United Nations. One of the obstacles to proper Chinese representation in the United Nations has been the opposition of the United States. Until recent years, the government of the United States has been a prisoner of American public opinion on the question. Because the American public would not allow its government to acquiesce in the representation of Red China in the U.N., American public opinion has been a factor in the failure to thoroughly control nuclear power. Therefore, I concentrated on this topic as one step toward a sane worldwide nuclear policy.

ACKNOWLEDGMENT

This study was originally written as a graduate thesis at Boston College, Chest nut Hill, Massachusetts, under the title *United States Opposition to the Represen tation of the People's Republic of China in the United Nations.* I am grateful t the authorities at Boston College for permission to publish the manuscript.

The work is primarily intended to be an appeal to American public opinion o the question. A number of people helped me in the writing, and I wish t acknowledge my gratitude to them. Miss Marion Van Schagen, of Canton, served a first editor and typist. My aunt, Miss Alice Reynolds, also of Canton, proofread th manuscript.

At Boston College, Professor Peter S. H. Tang was particularly helpful a faculty adviser. In addition, Professor Gary P. Brazier extended a welcomed hand The following gentlemen at Boston College were also of assistance—R. J. Cahill M. P. Fontaine, T. H. O'Connor and R. K. Woetzel.

C.V.R., JR

Wellesley, Massachusetts
19 April 1970

INTRODUCTION

C. V. Reynolds' book is of the kind that our age needs perhaps more than any other. It is not only exceptionally timely, full of common sense, and inspired throughout with a profound sense for justice and fair play but it has also an ardent desire to say the right thing, to inject some morality into politics, and to serve the common good. It does not enjoin us to appease "aggressors," but speaks in the best interests of the United States.

If Reynolds' book were read, understood, and remembered by sufficiently large numbers of people, it could save the U.S. treasury hundreds of billions of good dollars and the American people blood, sweat and tears over many years to come. On the other hand, if that measure of reason for which Reynolds argues does not soon prevail, a catastrophe may befall us in comparison with which the Vietnamese debacle would fade into utter insignificance. At the start of the Vietnam war, U.N. Secretary-General U Thant warned: "The pressure of events is remorselessly leading toward a major war, while efforts to revise that trend are lagging disastrously behind. In my view, the tragic error is being repeated of relying on force and military means in a deceptive pursuit of peace."

Since the United Nations was founded to maintain peace the world has seen nothing but war, cold war and hot war: war in the Middle East, Africa, war in Korea, Vietnam, Laos, Cambodia . . . ever present, ever threatening, ever widening war. In recent years the world spent $160 billion for military purposes annually—the single largest spender being the U.S.—while in the developing nations sixty-four per cent of the population lives on less than $100 a year—in misery, squalor, ignorance and filth.

What then is the United Nations really good for? Is there anything wrong with it? We submit that there is nothing wrong with the *idea* but plenty with its structure, organization, and the psychological constitution of its members. Let us look at the facts: the United Nations are idsmally *dis*united; the Security Council breeds insecurity; the organization is based on the principle of "sovereign *equality*" (Charter Art. 2, 1) of all its members, while the institution of the veto (Art. 27, 3) eloquently demonstrates their *inequality*. Some nations are so huge and powerful that they have put the U.N. on the shelf, arrogating its rights and functions to themselves, while other nations are so tiny that practically nobody but they themselves know or care about their membership. On the other hand, and paradoxically, China—one quarter of mankind, by far the largest of all nations—is excluded. Does this make sense?

It does not seem so, especially if one considers that not one of the really crucial international problems, such as nuclear test suspension, nuclear weapons manufacture, general disarmament, world population control, development in developing countries, or the conflict in Vietnam, can be attacked effectively without mainland China's participation. China, because of its size, its enormous and industrious population, its age-old civilization, and, today, its growing atomic power, is a world problem which needs the most careful attention not merely for China's sake alone but for that of all other nations as well.

The Chinese dragon, resenting years of maltreatment, is aroused. It is belching nuclear smoke. It will not be long before it will be breathing nuclear fire. Someone is going to be burned if steps are not taken to avert a nuclear doomsday. These necessary steps will not be taken, however, if China is not understood: the vastness of its problems, the depth of its frustration.

For over a hundred years China was robbed of her territories, of her resources, and even of her time-honored ideals by foreign encroachments and successive wars. From 1840 to 1945 China was attacked, stamped on, humiliated and fleeced by one foreign country after another. "A century of such treatment," in the words of Arnold Toynbee, "would be enough to make a saint turn savage."

Before her great fall, China was the greatest power on earth, the only great power in Asia. There are few nations as proud as the Chinese; even fewer have better reason for their pride. Any Chinese leadership is bound to be antagonistic as long as another great power has military bases next door to China and maintains impregnable naval and air supremacy in Chinese seas. Unless America's public opinion forces our government to withdraw from the Asian mainland and islands directly adjacent to it, war seems inevitable between China and the United States. Threatened China has long prepared for this war and gets more ready for it every passing day. She is now already fighting it by proxy on its peripheries from Korea to norther Thailand. The Chinese are well aware of their strength and of America's weakness: its military and emotional overcommitment in Asia. They envision a long, gradually expanding non-nuclear war that will drag on and on until America is tired, exhausted, hopelessly divided.

Military observers point to the fact that China's men of military age, ninety million strong, are three times the number of that in the U.S. As to nuclear power, the Communist Chinese are believed* to be able to launch an attack of two dozen or more nuclear-tipped missiles on the U.S. this year or next. True, in 1964, after acquiring nuclear weapons, the Chinese announced that they would not use them first; on the other hand, the fear of retaliation, the risk of uncontrolled fallout and the very destructiveness of U.S. nuclear power makes its use by America practically impossible.

*Statement by Secretary of Defense Laird, Feb. 24, 1970.

In addition to the enormity of its manpower and possibility of nuclear retaliation, there are still other military and geopolitical factors favoring China: whereas Uncle Sam lives almost 10,000 miles away on another continent, whereas the Soviet Union has its main centers of industry and population in Central Europe and India is cut off from East Asia by the mountain wall of the Himalayas, China, lying on the same continental shelf as the small Buddhist countries south of its border and having an enormous periphery, hence compelling enemies to disperse their forces, China, indeed, enjoys all the geostrategic advantages of inner communications. Therefore, when it comes to fighting localized wars in neighboring countries, not to speak of the defense of her own territory, China is virtually indestructible. Moreover, not only China with unbreakable racial, historical and cultural ties in the region is itself invincible, but the small nations China chooses to support and prods to fight us in a war by proxy are "invincible" as well. This, by the way, is one of the expensive lessons our bitter experience in Korea and Vietnam ought to have taught us by now.

Considering these circumstances and also the different foundations on which Chinese behavior, including their conduct in foreign affairs, is based, we cannot expect China to respond to our approaches in the way we hope. The West has only two choices: either we can ignore China and allow the gulf between ourselves and one quarter of mankind to widen, or else we can try to help it find a place in the sun commensurate with its size and importance. The latter policy would involve a search for ways to articulate the fact that the West respects China, respects Chinese civilization, and respects Chinese territory. To refuse China entry into the United Nations and other international bodies, to refuse to enter into diplomatic relations with it, to maintain the myth that Chiang Kai-shek still governs the Chinese mainland, and to ignore China's historical experience and social traditions is to impede the process of mutual understanding and of reconciliation which we must seek in our own best interest.

China's eagerness for scientific and technological progress, for overall modernization and an accepted place in the international community are a near guarantee for a change of its policy if ours would fundamentally change. Halfhearted reconciliatory gestures will be of no avail. If the Chinese become really convinced that there is a change of heart and purpose on the part of their foes, they will gradually respond. Their word for politics is *cheng* which means correct conduct, straightening out what is crooked, or bringing about conformity with what is intrinsically fair and just. The Chinese word for peace is *ho-ping*. Translated literally, it means food for all, as food and peace are inextricably intertwined.

The United Nations was created to maintain peace with justice in international affairs. If political differences are discussed within the U.N. framework it means, to quote the late Dag Hammerskjold, that "the United Nations Charter as a whole emerges as a background of the deliberations. It means that the negotiating parties accept as guiding them those basic rules of international coexistence, of which the Charter is an expression." The harshness of unilateral negotiations between hostile powers is thereby greatly mitigated and political doors can open which otherwise would remain closed. It is in this context that the anxious question which Reynolds asks becomes inescapable: "Why not admit Red China to the United Nations?"

University of Utah   HELMUT G. CALLIS

CHAPTER I

CRUX OF THE PROBLEM
IMPERIALISM VS. COMMUNISM

It has been United States strategy to oppose admitting Peking's representatives to the United Nations. This was not always the case.

After Mao proclaimed the People's Republic of China in the fall of 1949, the United States Government was ready to write off its participation in the Chinese Civil War. Public opinion in the United States was hostile to China. However, there was no overpowering fear of China which was to come later. Had there been no Korean War, it is not unlikely that China would have been a United Nations member in five years, and recognized by the United States Government within a decade.

Russia recognized the new regime on 20 October, 1949. The United States Department of State promised not to recognize China until it consulted Congress. Britain was inclined to offer de facto recognition.

During the summer of 1949, the U. S. Government wrote off Nationalist China as a lost cause. The U. S. State Department White Paper, issued on 5 August, 1949, stated that the Kuomintang under Chiang had sunk into such ineptitude and corruption that it had lost the support of the Chinese people. Dean Acheson thought that eventually China would throw off the Communist rule. Acheson said that the United States would always encourage developments in China toward establishing a liberal, non-Communist government.[1]

The Chinese Communist bid for United Nations recognition came in the fall of 1949. China was governed by Peking and not by Taiwan. Therefore, both the Russians and the Chinese Communists thought the credentials of Nationalist Delegate, T. F. Tsiang, were no longer valid.[2]

On 23 November, Russia informed the U. N. General Assembly that it no longer recognized the Nationalists' right to represent China in the United Nations. Russia's Jacob Malik walked out of the U. N. Security Council on 13 January, 1950 when the Council refused to immediately oust the delegation from Nationalist China.

In a speech to the National Press Club, on 12 January, 1950, Secretary of State Acheson stated that the essence of United States policy toward China was as follows: there was nothing the United States could do militarily about Communism in Asia. We would fight only to defend Japan, Okinawa, and the Philippines.

The new nations of South Asia were on their own. The United States could not impose on them the will to fight Communism. The United States must keep its hands off Asia, except where its economic guidance was invited. If there was a fighting chance that these nations could emerge from an era of social ferment without turning to Communism, then the United States should answer requests for economic aid and advice.[3]

The Korean War changed all this. On 1 August, 1950, Russia returned to the Security Council. It had lost its chance to veto United Nations action in Korea by its boycott. Jacob Malik assumed the Chairmanship for August. When he tried to bar the Chinese Nationalists by a ruling from the Chair, United States Ambassador Austin challenged the ruling. Most Council members held that the Chinese question should be decided by the General Assembly.[4]

Usually a Chinese Communist speaker will harangue against the United States as an imperialistic, war-mongering aggressor. Unfortunately, China has singled out the United States as its primary enemy. No doubt this is mainly due to United States assistance to Chiang during the Civil War. However, China and the United States had been traditional allies, or, at least friends, not enemies. When other countries of the world were carving out special areas of self-interest in China, the United States was proclaiming its 'open-door' policy.

When John Hay became American Secretary of State, in 1898, he did not know much about Far Eastern affairs. Nor did he understand human nature. He could see that the European powers and Japan were ready to carve up China permanently. Some circles dismiss Hay as unrealistic, and, in a way, hypocritical. His critics say he wanted other nations to let go of their hard-won advantages and open the door to American trade. Nevertheless, the American policy was better for China than the policy of the Europeans.

Over the last century and one-half of Chinese history, the United States appears as the foremost Western friend of China. Why, then, is there such fear, hatred, and recrimination between China and the United States? China talks of the imperialistic United States. We, in America, talk of Chinese imperialism. Of course, we do not use those words, but that is what we mean when we cite the example of China as an aggressive country which is trying to foster international wars of liberation throughout the world. This is the source of friction and the heart of the problem. It is an issue of Imperialism and not Communism.

Imperialism historically has been the act of a state in seeking to control areas outside its borders. In contrast, Communism is an ideology which proclaims an international utopian society where state governments will be so unnecessary that they will wither away from disuse. Plato and St. Thomas More thought along similar lines. Confucius, too, was materialistic. He did not complicate his philosophy with thought of heaven, hell, or a supreme being. To him the good life was an an end in itself, just as knowledge to Cardinal Newman was an end in itself. Communism, morally speaking, is theoretically indifferent, neither intrinsically good nor evil.

Let us look at the basic problem. It is not Communism which is to be feared, but Imperialism and Imperialism can take many forms. It can be Russian Imperialism; French Imperialism, as practiced by Napoleon; German Imperialism as practiced by Hitler; or Economic Imperialism, as practiced by the laissez-faire school of rugged individualists in the United States, including the 'Robber Barons,' Jay Cooke and Company. Imperialism is found among all peoples. Communism is a system of government which has been used to further imperialistic ambitions. The colonial powers of Western Europe were not Communistic, but they were Imperialistic. Imperialism flourishes under Communism, Constitutional Monarchy, and Democracy.

Winston Churchill is a heroic figure, not because he was a British Imperialist, but because he was both an active man, and a thinker who made mistakes, learned his lessons, and then led his people to victory against a ruthless enemy. If Churchill had been successful at Gallipoli, might there have been no Russian Revolution, and, thus, no International Communist Movement? No. After all, even if the Russia of the czars had stayed intact and had continued to be an ally of the Western Powers after the Kaiser was defeated, would that Russia have lasted long? Surely it would have fallen a decade and one-half later during the Great Depression. A lesson of history, which is always evident, but never learned, is that neither governments nor peoples learn their lessons unless they learn the hard way. Each one of us will go out and learn our own bitter lesson, rather than heed the advice of our elders. So it was with the Russian czars, and with men of privilege everywhere. They would not give in or reform until blood had been shed and in many cases, until it was too late. After the French Revolution, the returning French Emigrés had learned nothing and forgotten nothing. Even the French Revolution did not teach a lasting lesson. Those who do not know history are doomed to repeat it.

Most of us would agree that some of the progress which has been made in the field of social justice should be attributed to the Communist dialectic. The French Revolution was, no doubt, more violent than the Russian Revolution of 1917, and after the final defeat of Napoleon and the French Empire, Wellington and Metternich were so horrified by its excesses that they lost interest in reform and strove to create a balance of power. This was quite successful. We had a *Pax Britannica* for about a century. The "Concert of Europe," during the nineteenth cetury, played a leading part in the development of instruments for international consultation and compromise. The Congress of Vienna, however, was motivated by reaction, not reform. The century of world peace resulted primarily from two things—the strength of the British Fleet and the concept of Britannia ruling the waves. Later,

Britain followed with an enlightened colonial policy. However, Britain, the source of our ancient political liberties, has been the power which most frequently has violated freedom of the seas. Denial of freedom on the seas was a form of Imperialism.

In the last two generations, the United States and the world have benefited from the forces of international Communism, particularly after World War II, but also during the Great Depression. During the Depression it would not have been possible to introduce New Deal social reforms and government controls, but for the specter of Communism. Rugged individualism with the accent on corporate and personal greed had gone wild during the 1920's. Capitalism had almost gone to its own destruction at its own hand, as Marx and Engels had predicted. However, the salvation came as reform from within. The election of 1932 brought reform into the government.

Would it have been possible for President Roosevelt to push through his program of the one hundred days if the Congress did not fear Communism? The alternative to government action was a worsening depression. This was a good climate for Communist agitators to work. The presence of a Soviet Russia and a strong International Communist Movement was a blessing in disguise. Without it our Government would have had difficulties carrying out its program of necessary reform.

After World War II, Russian Imperialism was on the march, and International Communism was its tool. The United States met it with the Marshall Plan. A healthy economy in Western Europe meant a strong North Atlantic Community. Strong economies helped governments counter Communism by eliminating much of the poverty and injustice where Communism flourished.

Perhaps even Castro's Communism in Cuba is a blessing in disguise. To counter it, we have engaged in an Alliance for Progress. Aid in this case is linked with attempts at internal social reform, thus penetrating to the heart of the problem in Latin America. The poverty resulting from centuries of privilege for the few, and nothing for the masses, is being fought with land reform.

Soviet missiles in Cuba during the fall of 1962 were tools of Russian Imperialism, not of Castro's Communism. It is likely that they would not have been there at all if the United States had not supported dictators such as Fulgencio Batista in return for economic privileges to United States companies operating in Cuba.

Imperialism must be contained. In addition, an alliance between Christians and Marxists against materialistic forces in both East and West is vital to the world. This is the view of Dr. Machovec, a Marxist Professor of Philosophy at Charles University, in Prague, Czechoslovakia. At first, such a dialogue might seem strange. However, it has begun. Probably the start could be traced to John XXIII and de-Stalinization in the Soviet Union. The Vatican seems to be making efforts to ease ideological tensions by co-operating with some Communist regimes. Such co-operation is infrequent, but the stand of the Church is radically different now than it was two decades ago in the days of Pope Pius XII. The dangers of a nuclear war have drawn together Christians and Marxists. Both Christians and Marxists are, after all, searching after the same thing—Marxists call it a stateless society, and Christians call it salvation. Dr. Machovec believes that Marxists could accept some parts of the Christian solution. For example, the Samaritan principle of helping one's neighbor is always valid. It does not differ ultimately very much from the Communist maxim of to each according to his need and from each according to his ability.

Dr. Machovec stated that the Soviet-led invasion in August, 1968, had made dialogue with Christians in Czechoslovakia more difficult. He expressed confidence, however, that it cannot be stopped.[5] If one wants to take a broad-minded look at things, one can come to the conclusion that Christ, Marx, and Confucius were all looking for the same thing—goodness.

FOOTNOTES

[1]*New York Times*, 6 August, 1949, p. 1
[2]*New York Times*, 16 November, 1949, p. 1
[3]Facts on File, Vol. X, 1950, p. 9
[4]*Ibid.* p. 243.
[5]*New York Times*, 23 February, 1969, p. 30

CHAPTER II

CHINA IN WORLD HISTORY

The Peking man of pre-Confucian China has been a great find to paleontologists. It is also of great value to the present regime, as it substantiates Chinese claims to superiority. The discovery of the Peking man indicates strongly the existence of human beings with an Old Stone Age Culture in China at least one-half million years ago. In certain respects, the Chinese have always considered themselves as something of a great find to the rest of the human race. During the Western Chou Dynasty of 1000 B.C., the Chinese communities thought themselves surrounded and interspersed with less cultured tribes. These neighbors were "barbarians," just as the United States imperialists and all their running dogs are the common enemy of all the people of the world, and particularly of the great, glorious and correct Communist People of China.[1]

The centuries before Christ were golden years of philosophy in China as in Greece. Chinese philosophy taught that man was part of a harmonious universe governed by transcendent law. Oriental moralists held that man would find his best ethical guide in his own nature. Aristotle preached the same thing, but he was more practical than the Chinese. The "Philosopher" of St. Thomas Aquinas counseled the cultivation of the golden mean. Virtue was nothing but a mean between extremes.

Confucius taught that clear thinking and self-discipline led the superior man to correct action in all his relationships.

Through moral influence and education, the superior man should lead the common herd with kindliness, justice, paternalism and the Golden Rule. Mencius urged China, by exemplary conduct, to win the world. Chairman Mao is not dissimilar in his counsels to the Chinese People and to the International Communist Movement.

The civilization of China begun about a thousand years after the establishment of civilizations in the Valley of the Indus continued into the twentieth century with many of its essential features intact. Where other cultures changed radically, Far-Eastern cultures changed slowly.

During most of her history, China has kept Imperialism under control. The great philosophers of China have exerted a pacifist influence. Until recent centuries, China did not have aggressive, organized states on her borders. Generally, the Chinese people have considered others as inferiors, but still as members of one great family. The Chinese seldom provoked surrounding countries. Present Chinese militancy stems from abuse which China has suffered recently, particularly during the 19th and 20th centuries.

Around 1500 B.C., portions of the Yellow River Valley were occupied by people of Mongolian stock who had passed from the Neolithic into the Bronze Age. The Shang Dynasty ruled in Bronze-Age China. The basic pattern for Chinese society and culture was established. It would seem, therefore, that the most influential Far-Eastern civilization was indigenous from the start. In certain respects, Chinese civilization was simple, but it had highly developed areas also. Systematic astronomical observations were made during the Shang Dynasty, and mathematics was developed along the decimal system.

Agriculture was the chief source of livelihood of the Shang people. Grains were the principal crops, especially wheat. Rice was also grown. This early civilization possessed a system of writing. Government power was vested in a royal family, but on the death of the King, the Crown passed to his younger brother in preference to the King's own sons. The King was assisted by an educated class of priests. The basic social institution was the family. Ancestor worship was already in existence.

Around the first millenium B.C., the Chou warriors overpowered the Shang Dynasty. The Chou people appreciated the greatness of the Shang culture and continued it. The Shang royal line was not entirely extinguished. Probably there was a fear of provoking powerful Shang ancestral spirits. The new dynasty yearned for legitimacy. It almost seems as if the Chou rulers had read John Locke. Claims were made that the last Shang ruler had been incompetent and debauched, and that it was correct for him to be replaced by a better person who was, of course, a Chou. In other ways, too, the Chou operated according to the principles of Locke.

The Chou developed the concept of governmental power as a commission from Heaven, rather than an absolute and inalienable right. This theme may have been invented for propaganda purposes. But it became a persistent element in Chinese political history.

The ruling house of the early Chou Dynasty declined in the 8th century B.C. The decline was so absolute that the nobles overthrew it in 771 B.C. Extravagant waste was a characteristic of King Yu, the last of the Western Chou Kings. Revolting nobles placed the son of the murdered King Yu on the throne. During the 500 years of the Eastern Chou Dynasty, China suffered political disunity and internal strife. Hereditary nobles enjoyed power, social prominence and wealth. This was a type of feudal society, but not Western, because a lesser aristocracy constituted a kind of middle class.

Around the middle of the fifth century B.C., internal conditions in China became extremely chaotic, inaugurating a bloody period of warring states. In spite of internal conflicts, cultural progress was almost continuous. This was the classic period of Chinese civilization. The contributions of this period were fundamental to the subsequent history of the Far East and of the world.

Confucius has proved to be one of history's most influential men. By normal standards, his life was largely a failure, yet he left an indelible stamp upon the thought and political institutions of China. Confucius showed a sincere interest in the common people, and did not choose his disciples on the basis of birth or rank. He was, in a sense, a drifter. He wandered from ruler to ruler, looking for some one who would give him a chance to apply his ideals and thus set in motion a tide of reform which might sweep the entire country.

Confucius, like Socrates, made his contribution as a teacher. Like Socrates, and like his contemporary Buddha, Confucius believed that knowledge was the key to happiness and successful conduct.

In the time of Confucius, philosophers were active in three widely separated regions of the ancient world. While the Greeks were inquiring into the nature of the physical universe, and Indian thinkers were pondering the value of pain and the relationship of the soul to the Absolute Being, Chinese sages were attempting to discover the basis of human society and the underlying principles of good government.

The doctrines of Confucius centered upon the good life and the good community. He stressed propriety and the observance of the ceremonial forms, which he thought were helpful in acquiring self-discipline. However, he was really more concerned with sincerity and intelligence than with appearances. Confucius visualized the state as a benevolent paternalism. The ruler not only commanded, but also set an example for others to follow.

The Ch'in Dynasty, inaugurated after the overthrow of the Chou, lasted only fourteen years (221-207). It was a short but important dynasty, for it carried out the reorganization of the government, permanently effecting the character of the state. Shih Huang Ti, who founded this dynasty, was a man of iron will and administrative genius. He assumed the title of "First Emperor," did away with rival kingdoms, centralized administration, and eliminated the philosophic schools. Sections of the Great Wall were completed, strategic roads were constructed, and canals were built. But this monarch had an Achilles' heel. He was addicted to superstitious fancies, and undertook several journeys in search of the elixir of immortality. The dynasty ended in a round of court conspiracies and assassinations. The Ch'in rule carried into practice the harsh doctrines of coercion, punishment and fear, and bore a striking resemblance to the European totalitarian regimes of the twentieth century.

The Han Dynasty succeeded the Ch'in. As Chinese dynasties came and went, they tended to follow a similar course, and met with a similar fate. An ambitious person would usurp power. To be accepted as legitimate, however, a new dynasty had to promote general prosperity as well as defend the country and suppress internal strife. Look now at the trouble of Mao and the failure of the Great Proletarian Revolution. Historically, when a new dynasty failed to resolve the current crisis, it went down in bloodshed, and a new, firm hand seized control. The Han Rule was energetic, efficient, enlightened, but also severe. Chinese control over border areas was extended. In central Asia, sections of Tarim Basin and Turkestan were brought under control. In addition, southern Manchuria and northern Korea were annexed. Both in territory and power, China, under the Han, was almost equal to the contemporary Roman Empire. Chinese trading routes were extensive. Caravans traversed Sinkiang and Turkestan. The Chinese also began to travel the high seas. Chinese merchants exchanged produce not only with India and Ceylon, but also with Japan, Persia, Arabia, Syria, and indirectly with Rome. The leading Chinese export, silk, commanded a high price, so the balance of trade was favorable to China.

While Rome was supreme in the West, and Christ was beginning to be heard, the Hsin Dynasty was undertaking radical reforms in China. All candidates for office were required to take civil-service examinations. Land was nationalized, and large estates were divided among the peasantry. Regional commissions were established to stabilize prices. Surplus goods were purchased at cost. Even the market was pegged by sales above the seasonal index. Commercial relations were gradually extended through the Southern Seas. Sumatra and other island states sent traders and tribute to China.

China, like Rome, fell into periods of decline. The reasons were similar. Various rapacious rulers stimulated bitter opposition. Around the year 200 A.D., the Han Dynasty faded away. Actual power passed to competing military dictators. Taoism developed from the insecurity of property and life in the years after the passing of the Han Dynasty. This cult of mysticism promised a kind of immortality as a reward for faith. These teachings were similar to those of Christ and the developing Church of Rome. Buddhism began to flourish in China after the close of the Han Dynasty. It proved irresistible, with its novel conceptions, with the ideal of nirvana, and with the promise of eventual salvation.

Although the dates are not identical, the period of political disunity following the Han Dynasty is comparable to the time of confusion in Europe after the Fall of the Roman Empire. The Han State had been a practical and effective expression of Chinese experience. It utilized existing social and economic institutions, and emphasized ancient traditions. This period of semi-anarchy, therefore, did not destroy China's civilization. The Chinese fiber showed through, regardless of raging political controversies.

After four centuries of disunity in Medieval China, there followed another vigorous and highly successful dynasty, the Tang (600-900). The Tang Dynasty developed in China at the same time as the expansion of Islam in the Mediterranean area, and the rise of feudalism in Western Europe. Military conquests during the seventh century brought China into stimulating contacts with Iranian and Indian civilizations. The Chinese emperors, although conquerors, were liberal and tolerant, as well as being patrons of the arts. Chinese suzerainty was acknowledged by the petty states of Western and Eastern Turkestan. Religious Taoism also received royal support. Contact by sea between China, Sumatra and India became highly developed. Chinese scholars began to learn Sanskrit. The following century in China was one of brilliant literary and artistic achievement. The Chinese Renaissance predated the Renaissance of the West by at least half a millenium. The Tang Dynasty in many respects marked the culmination of China's cultural evolution.

The Tang hegemony over Central Asia was imposing, but it could not last long. With the rapid expansion of Islam, the Chinese Empire was ultimately unable to resist. The Arabs gained control of Turkestan. The religion of Islam was bequeathed to that area as a permanent heritage. The Tang Rulers also encountered trouble with Tibet. From time to time, the Tibetans invaded Chinese territory and allied themselves with the Turks and Arabs in attempts to block trade between China and Persia through the Pamir Mountains. For about fifty years following the collapse of the great Tang Dynasty in the early tenth century, China was a divided country with power in the hands of military dictators. After a brief interregnum, known as the Period of the Five Dynasties, a strong, central government was established by an able general who assumed the imperial title and founded the Sung Dynasty.

The Sung Dynasty of China appeared approximately the same time as the Cluniac Movement in Western Europe. In China this was an age of humanism, of scholar-statesmen who were at once poets, artists, and philosophers. China had its Leonardo da Vinci, its Aristotle, its Michelangelo, its Erasmus, and its Thomas Jefferson before the "renaissance man" concept had been imprinted in Western minds. The thirteenth century marked the advent of modernity in China, not only in social organization, but in humanism, art, literature, belief, and philosophy. Eastern maritime commerce swelled in the 11th century, as Arabs entered into competition with Persians at Canton. Trade in cotton goods brought, in addition, Jewish traders from Persia and India.

Buddhism developed in the centuries of the Sung. Early Chinese philosophers had been primarily concerned with ethics. Now there was a shift from the study of right acting to the study of right thinking. The accent shifted from ethics to epistemology, the study of the nature of certitude; and to the study of ontology, the study of that which may be, whether it is or not. The achievement of the Sung philosophers was to achieve a synthesis between ancient ethics and the new rationalized metaphysics. A Chinese predecessor to Cardinal Newman stressed that knowledge was essential to self-improvement. Without knowledge, there would be no improvement of type, and no progress of human welfare. The Chinese medieval synthesis developed the concept of a just, impersonal and benevolent Heaven. Great stress was placed on the teachings of Mencius, who had emphasized that goodness springs from within.

In central Asia, after the thirteenth century, a new Empire, that of the Mongols, developed and rapidly expanded. It used in this expansion military strategy plus discipline, mobility, espionage and terror. The Mongol invaders were led primarily by Kublai Khan. His capital was built where Peking now stands, and his empire stretched from the Pacific Ocean to Europe. The most famous European visitor to it was Marco Polo.

The Ming Dynasty was established in 1368 by Chinese Nationalists eager to rid their land of the foreigner. By 1382, the Mongols were driven out of China, and the whole territory of China was under Chinese control. During the early periods of the fifteenth century, just as Henry V was about to embark on an expedition which almost extinguished French sovereignty, a series of Chinese naval expeditions were launched. The Chinese desired commerce, wealth, and military prestige. Expeditions set out from Chinese ports which touched the countries of the South Seas, Annam, Ceylon, the Near East, and Africa. The ships were armed with cannon and forced the payment of tribute on occasion. Cities and states as far away as Mecca acknowledged the might of China. Tribute came in money as well as in horses, copper ore, sulfur, drugs, timber and spices.

During the second half of the 16th century, Chinese emperors seemed not to show comparable interest in foreign adventures. This was unfortunate for China, because Europe was then emerging as many aggressive sea-power states. In China a spirit of isolationism spread in Court circles. The sixteenth century, the great century of Spain and Portugal, saw repeated encroachments on Chinese soil. The Portugese and the Japanese invaded coastal areas, while Moslems made excursions into the western frontier. Japan attempted to invade via Korea. By this time, China's economic strain was becoming severe. Imperial leadership was lax. Morale at Peking and in the field deteriorated. When the Manchus rose in strength, north of the Great Wall, they were able to take Peking, the ancient capital city. The Mings were driven south and eventually to Formosa.

With the disintegration of the Ming Dynasty, China succumbed, for the second time in her history, to conquest by a foreign invader. By the early seventeenth century, a strong military organization had been formed in the Amur River region by the Manchus. The Manchus took advantage of China's weakness and factional strife at about the same time as Cromwell was winning the Battle of Marston Moor. To make their domination clear to all, the Manchus imposed the partly shaven head and queue on every man. Peace, beginning finally in 1683, about the same time as the Glorious Revolution in England, made possible careful administration and judicious control. Foreign adventurers were repressed. The Portugese were allowed to remain in Macao, but were not permitted elsewhere.

The Russians, pushing out across Siberia, challenged the Manchus in their northern homeland. But by the Treaty of Nerchinsk, in 1689, the Russians agreed to desist from force. A Jesuit negotiator, Jean-Francois Gerbitton, advised the Russians to abandon military pressure for commercial penetration. Of all the foreigners at the Manchu Court, the most tolerated were the Jesuits. They were men of scholarship, well-versed in both the Chinese and Manchu languages, who introduced the Emperor to certain branches of European learning. The Jesuits performed numerous services, assisting as interpreters in state business involving Europeans, preparing maps, establishing the calendar, and even curing the Emperor of malaria.

Materially, the Manchu Dynasty was very successful. The state included Manchuria, Mongolia, Sinkiang, and Formosa, while Tibet was a protectorate; and Korea, Burma, Nepal and parts of Indo-China were tributary dependencies. During the first half of the Dynasty's history, the government was remarkably efficient. While Europe was in a condition of turbulence and shaken by wars of rival despots during the eighteenth century, China enjoyed the advantages of unity and peace under a government which was at least stable. China, in this century, was one of the best governed and most highly civilized states in the world. It was also the largest in territory and in the number of its inhabitants.

From the outset, the Manchus attempted to identify themselves with old Chinese culture and institutions. The Chinese subjects were ruled in accordance with accepted traditions. Civil-service examinations were continued, the ancient administrative framework was preserved, and the state cult of Confucius was exalted.

But under the Manchus, China began to feel acute distress from the rapid growth in population. Nothing equivalent to an industrial revolution had occurred, and numerous economic and social changes created problems. The lack of sufficient arable land led to clearing and cropping areas in the upper river valleys. Deforestation eventually produced soil erosion and increased the danger of floods and droughts.

In addition, a cloud began to disturb the relations of the Jesuits with Peking. Papal and Imperial authority clashed over the Chinese name for God, and the acceptability of Chinese rites. The Jesuits, practical as always, had accepted Chinese rites toward Heaven, Confucius and their ancestors. At Rome, the archenemies of the Jesuits, that is, other churchmen, thought that Jesuits had been too Jesuitical. It was charged that the Jesuits had dabbled in intrigue for succession in concert with adult sons. This was probably at least partially true. At any rate, it did the Jesuits no good. The Chinese victor in the power struggle became hostile to the Jesuits, as one would be to any potential king-maker. The end of the active Jesuit Mission to the Manchu Court came in 1782.

Within Chinese society, there were other signs of dissatisfaction, despite, or, perhaps because of, military successes abroad and the extended era of peace at home. Reserves in the Treasury were dissipated. However, the Arts flourished. The Emperor was a patron of the Arts and a scholar, as well as an administrator. Desiring to leave a large library behind him, all rare books in public and private hands were collected. Many of them turned out to be critical (of the Emperor), and they were burned, deleted, or hidden. A number of critical scholars suffered the extreme penalty, because the Emperor considered criticism intolerable. Later on, toward old age and senility, Ch'ien-lung allowed himself to be corrupted by a sycophant who won his confidence, and then went on to corrupt the Civil Service. Liberty seems to have declined as the Arts flourished.

From this point, the Manchu Dynasty deteriorated swiftly. Book-burning, and the reluctance to suffer criticism, hastened the decline. Revolts broke out in China, just as the British were about to begin their struggle against Napoleon.

Trade in opium had been forbidden in 1729. However, within a century, and particularly after 1820, importation grew alarmingly with Chinese and foreign connivance. In the Portugese harbor of Macao, there were also French, Dutch, British and American ships. Merchants were eager to make a quick profit. Tea, silk, and cotton goods were purchased in Canton, in exchange for spice and opium. The purchase of opium meant an unfavorable balance of trade for China.

Around 1821, the trade in Indian opium was transferred to an island off the Canton River. Foreign tradesmen were eager to buy and sell on their own terms, and make a quick profit. They were irked by various restrictions. It was necessary to deal with an officially established group of petty local officials. The absence of a fixed tariff, and the venality of the officials had led to strong protests against trade at Canton. Trade conditions at Canton had become intolerable because of local official arbitrariness. There were recurrent conflicts of interest, restrictions on personal freedom, and denial of appeal to the central government.

The Manchus were unwilling to permit official intercourse on the basis of equality. At first, the Russians received more favorable treatment at Peking than did other foreigners. Gradually, the trading nations of the West demanded better terms for themselves. Portugese, Dutch, and British missions traveled to Peking. But the Chinese were not accustomed to dealing with other governments on an equal basis, and regarded all foreigners as the bearers of tribute. Something had to break. The West was expanding, the Napoleonic Wars were over, and industrial Europe wanted markets and raw materials. This was also the period of the clipper-ship trade with the United States. The United States had entered the profitable China trade within a year of its independence.

Pressure came from Britain first. In 1834, the monopoly of the East India Company ended. This monopoly had been very important in the Canton system of commercial regulation. Lord Napier became the British Superintendent of Trade in Canton. Chinese officials refused to deal with him as an equal. Napier was simply a head merchant. The British merchants continued to demand more concessions than the Chinese were ready to concede. British and Chinese ideas of international trade were fundamentally opposed to each other. The British thought in terms of British-Imperial Masters and subject-trading peoples. The Chinese thought in terms of Chinese superiority and inferior-trading barbarians.

The conflicts reached a breaking point on opium. Of course, the trade was outlawed, but it was profitable. Therefore, it existed. Foreign merchants brought in ever-increasing quantities to China, and corrupt Manchu officials connived in the trade. Finally, around 1840, the Chinese decided to stop the traffic with a show of force.

The British objected to what were considered high-handed measures, and in November, 1839, hostilities broke out. Within a year, the British had occupied Canton River forts. Under the Treaty of Nanking, in 1842, Hong Kong was ceded to the British. Five ports were opened to foreign residence and to trade with consular supervision (Canton, Shanghai, Foochow, Ningpo, and Amoy). Within a year, a "fair and regular tariff" was agreed upon. The British, having won the war, received most-favored-nation treatment.

Things did not run smoothly after 1843. The foreigners did not think they had won enough concessions. The Chinese believed that they had conceded too much. Furthermore, since the concessions had been given under duress, responsible authorities felt no moral obligation to live up to them. The Chinese were no further inclined than formerly to treat Western barbarians as equals. Clashes were frequent, and the illegal, profitable trade in opium continued. For a decade, the Western Powers took offense easily and used minor incidents to extract more concessions from China. Under the Treaty of Tientsin, between China and Britain, France, the United States, and Russia, eleven more ports were opened to foreigners. Christian missions were permitted in the interior. Foreign legations were to be permitted at Peking. However, the Chinese refused to actually admit foreign diplomats to Peking. Just as America was preparing for the election of Lincoln and the great blood bath of the American Civil War, British and French Troops, 17,000 strong, occupied Peking. The Conventions increased indemnities and Western privileges. The Russians secured cessions, also, and founded Vladivostok.

Occidentals may be overwhelmed by Chinese statements of vitriolic hatred. The hatred is easier to understand when we consider that the various treaty concessions between 1842 and 1860 served as the legal basis for intercourse between China and the West until World War II. These treaties seemed to solve troublesome situations at the time, but they were a violation of Chinese sovereignty, and really threatened the existence of the state. Foreigners in China were removed from Chinese jurisdiction; Westerners regulated the tariffs; and Christian missions were granted imperial authority within the interior of China.

It is not surprising that there were internal revolts within China. Secret societies, strongly anti-Manchu, thrived in South China. The illegal trade in opium encouraged gangsters, just as illegal trade in liquor in the America of the Twenties encouraged gangsterism. The Chinese people also suffered from severe famines. Banditry increased, disorder spread, and uprisings were almost inevitable. Various rebel groups in the interior, unable to provide conquered territory with either protection or constructive administration, were foredoomed to failure.

After 1860, the British continued to lead in the exploitation of China, with the Russians ready to take what they could. New ports occasionally were opened and foreign commerce grew. During earlier periods of domestic turmoil, the Manchu Government had allowed foreigners to collect internal maritime customs as a matter of convenience. The expedient was soon adopted at all ports, and soon the Imperial Maritime Customs Service came under the direction of an Occidental.

The Customs Service eventually became not only a collector of revenue, but responsible for charting and lighting the coast, and for the inaugurating of a postal system. Rebellions continued to threaten the power of the Manchus. Around 1860, the Manchu Dynasty, though destined to fail, took on a new lease on life. Some able Chinese came to its support. The Empress Dowager was unscrupulous, but vigorous. She ruled during the minority of her son, and was dominant, not only during his boyhood, but also after his accession. However, China could not hold back the onslaught for long.

During the last years of the 19th century the growing pressure of the West Japan began to take effect. A Japanese punitive expedition to Formosa, in 1874, exposed the weakness of the Chinese military. Japan, at the door of China, was rapidly adopting and adapting Western culture. Korea had long been a vassal state to China. Japan refused to recognize this special relationship. The two nations came to blows in 1894, when both tried to interfere in Korea. China was easily defeated. By 1895, the Japanese had successfully invaded Shantung and Manchuria, and had fortified posts which commanded the sea approaches to Peking. By the Treaty of Shimonoseki, China recognized the independence of Korea, and ceded Formosa and part of Manchuria (Liaotung Peninsula) to Japan. This last cession was bitterly opposed by Russia and France. Japan was forced to back down and forego acquiring Liaotung Territory, but still possessed Formosa. Japan's victory was actually a signal for other powers to join in the exploitation of China.

European powers scrambled for leases and other special privileges. This was the age of the new Imperialism in Europe. The Western powers were motivated by greed and by fear of one another. For a time, it almost seemed as if China would be partitioned permanently. Bankers vied with one another to lend the Chinese money with which to pay indemnities to the Japanese. France secured special territorial concessions in the Mekong River areas of Indo-China. Britain demanded and received concessions on the Burmese frontier. Germany moved into Shantung on a pretext and secured a harbor and mining concessions on favorable 99-year leasehold terms.

Along with these seizures and concessions, the great powers also marked out spheres of interest. These were implied rights to provide development capital in the various provinces of China. There was tremendous competition over the provision of capital for railways. Belgian financiers, working for French interests, provided railroad capital, as did Germans and certain Americans. Three major efforts were made to prevent the threatened disruption of China. One was by John Hay, of the United States—the "Open Door" Policy. The others were made by the Chinese themselves. After the war with Japan, various secret societies developed in China, advocating "reform" and Chinese organization on an Occidental pattern.

The other method advocated called for a return to the status quo, and elimination of reforms. In 1898 and 1899, unrest in China was widespread, partly because of Western aggression and partly because of vigorous reaction led by the Dowager Empress. The government, in an attempt to provide for the national defense, recruited trainloads of village militia. These groups came to be known as "Righteous Harmony Bands." The favorite motto of the groups, known to foreigners as "Boxers," was to protect the country and destroy the foreigner. By the fall of 1899, the Boxers were beginning to persecute Chinese Christians. Certain Western missionaries were killed during the winter. The storm finally broke in June of 1900, when the Dowager Empress ordered all foreigners to be killed. During the month of July, thousands of Occidentals were murdered. An international force responded, and Peking was captured on 14 August, 1900. The victors fought among themselves over how to punish China. It took a year to draw up the Boxer Protocol. This agreement was simply another case of Western insult and demands for apology and additional concessions and indemnities.

Educational, economic, and military reforms were undertaken in 1902. The defeat of Russia by Japan in 1904-1905 again revealed to China the advantages of learning from the West. After 1905, the Chinese set about reorganizing their country. They boycotted American goods as a protest against further exclusion of Chinese from America. A Ministry of Education was created, and Chinese students swarmed to Japan. A union of societies with the objective of ejecting the Manchus from China was organized in Japan by Sun Yat-sen.

Efforts were made to put the country in a better state of defense. Steps were taken in 1906 to create a national force, so that the state would no longer have to rely on the older provincial forces. Constitutional reform was also started in the first decade of the twentieth century. In 1909, provincial assemblies met, and within a year there was a National Assembly, half elected on a limited suffrage basis and half appointed by the Emperor.

In times of limited progress, demands increased. After 1900, a more radical movement began, aiming to overthrow the Manchu Dynasty. Ever since the 17th

Century, the Manchus had lived in comparative idleness. Through the 18th and 19th Centuries, the dynasty had been declining. The unsuccessful contests with foreign powers had shaken not only the dynasty, but the entire nation. The ferment of new ideas was weakening the feeble, old structure.

The actual events which led to the Revolution of 1912 were connected with railroad construction and finance. The government decided to take over a railroad in Szechwan. Construction had just begun. The amount offered to the stockholders was not acceptable to them. Chinese troops were called in to police the area. Dissatisfaction on both sides boiled over into open revolt. The troops mutinied, and the revolution was underway.

Dr. Sun Yat-sen returned from Japan. This prime figure among the radicals was born of a peasant family near Canton. He had obtained a Western education as a medical doctor in Hawaii. In 1895, Dr. Sun had participated in an abortive revolt. He was lucky to escape. Thereafter, he traveled widely in the West. He became convinced that Western institutions could be successfully adopted in China. He dedicated his energies to stirring up opposition to the Manchus. In China, this work was carried forward by a Secret Alliance Society. In December, 1911, one month after the railway outbreak, Dr. Sun returned from Europe and was elected President of the United Provinces of China by a revolutionary provisional assembly at Nanking. Dr. Sun resigned the following February in an attempt to unite the country.

Without much bloodshed or social upheaval, and without immediate interference by the great powers, both the Manchu Dynasty and the institution of the monarchy had been overthrown. However, these events proved to be only the beginning of the revolution. Any regime that succeeded the Manchus was confronted with the staggering problems of administrative corruption, economic stagnation, and general demoralization, the fruits of misrule for centuries. In addition, unequal treaties and foreign spheres of interest made a unified, modern state doubly difficult. Yuan Shih-K'ai had become the Provisional President of the Chinese Republic on the resignation of Sun Yat-sen. Yuan was more interested in personal power than in republican principles. At least Yuan was not a hypocrite. He believed in and practiced the Napoleonic scheme of obedience from below and authority from above.

Opposition parties were formed in 1912 in an attempt to curb his power. The Harmony of Progress Party of Liang Ch'i-ch'ao advocated a strong executive. The Chinese Nationalist Party (Kuo Min Tang of Dr. Sun Yat-sen) championed a system of parliamentary government. A constitution was drafted which placed limits on Yuan's power. Yuan was so successful in corrupting the members of the Parliament, however, that he was able to usurp power. He then contemptuously dissolved the assembly and ruled from 1914 until his death in 1916 as a military dictator. Western powers were quite willing to support a strong man in China as

long as China was weak. Russian intrigue combined with Mongol Nationalist sentiment to secure autonomy for Outer Mongolia. A rebellion in Tibet gave Britain a
chance to extend her influence in that development area. The Japanese were
casting covetous eyes on the German rights in Shantung.

After the death of Yuan, in 1916, much of China passed under the rule of
independent military commanders. China's participation in World War I brought
disaster. China could not even put her own house in order. The Peking government
had declared war against Germany in 1917, hoping to gain advantages at the peace
settlement. At the Paris Peace Conference, Mr. Wilson and his Fourteen Points
went with the wind. Japan, which had assisted her weak World War I ally, China,
by selling war materials and securing economic concessions, ended up with
Shantung at the Paris Peace Conference. Chinese revolutionaries then joined the
Communist Party and looked to Moscow for leadership against the double-crossing
Western devils and hypocrites.

FOOTNOTES

[1] Peking Review, Vol. II, No. 49, 6 December, 1968, p. 18

CHAPTER III

TRADITIONAL UNITED STATES-CHINA POLICY

The traditional American impression of China has not prepared us for a militant China of almost 800 million people. We, in the United States, have viewed the Chinese as exotic and dissimilar, and we are skeptical of them. This feeling seems to be increasing as we recognize Chinese nuclear capabilities. Our population is aware of the Chinese, and not a little afraid. We do not know what to expect, and, therefore, we expect the worst.

There has been another impression of China in the United States, one of admirable respect and almost reverence for the Chinese. When Doolittle raided Tokyo, American children thought that our fliers, who had to crashland in China, would surely be safe. These honest people were our friends and allies. There was no doubt at all that the Chinese would shelter Americans. China, in her valiant fight against the Japanese, was idealized in the American press. American mass psychology made a hero of Chiang Kai-shek, and a super heroine of Madame Chiang.

The official policy of the United States toward China has been contradictory. We went there to trade first; later, we were patronizing. The Yankee Clippers of New England were built for a fast, profitable China trade.

Shortly after the American Revolution, in December 1783, in the little five-ton sloop *Harriet* of Hingham, Captain Hallet sailed from Boston with a cargo of ginseng for China. Captain Hallett put in at the Cape of Good Hope. He met with some British East India men who, alarmed at Yankee competition, bought her cargo for double its weight in Hyson tea. Captain Hallett made a good bargain, but lost the honor of hoisting the first American ensign in Canton to a New York ship, the *Empress of China*.[1]

The *Empress of China* had New York capital and initiative, but it had a Yankee skipper from Boston, Major Samuel Shaw. Shaw arrived at Macao on 23 August, 1784, six months out of New York. Despite his inexperience, he brought home a cargo which stimulated competition. He established the first American commercial house in China at Canton in 1786, and China trade was born.[2]

As traders, we were quite junior to the British. This put us in quite an enviable position. We could trade and have the protection of the British Fleet, yet we could denounce British Imperialism. Usually, American policy acquiesced querulously in British policy.

The two different views of China and the fluctuations in our China policy probably account for the national hysteria on questions of China. In the 1930's, the Chinese were noble fighters, and during the war they were grand allies. Madame Chiang was a beautiful, gracious lady, educated at Wellesley, so her husband must be noble. The fact that he was an ally of Stalin for a time was never brought out forcefully, nor were his repressive measures against the peasants discussed. The war against the Communists was just as noble as the war which was being waged against Japan. The great power of the China lobby in the United States is testimony to this emotionalism. It does not seem possible now that the China lobby could have controlled two hundred Representatives in the United States Congress. How incredible it is now that Senator McCarthy could have had such success in denouncing General Marshall, and claiming that Chiang was sold down the river.

December 7 stands out in the minds of most Americans—Pearl Harbor and the humiliation of the United States Fleet. For the people of the Orient, it teaches a different lesson. This was the day to show the way. An Oriental power attacked a strong Western power and overwhelmed it. In a period of six months, a new empire had come under the control of Japan. This was a grand form of imperialism in reverse. It still shows the way to the Indonesians fighting against the Dutch; the Malaysians against the British; the Indo-Chinese against the French; and the Vietnamese against the Americans. They all look back to the memory of the Japanese victories and obtain inspiration.

The Japanese were finally defeated, but they did show how the West could be overwhelmed. It was a lesson learned well and used well in the fight against colonial powers after the Second World War. Not only for this reason is December 7th memorable. Eight years to the day after Pearl Harbor, the Nationalist Government of China fled the mainland and declared, on the next day, that Taipei, Taiwan, was their new capital city. The Chinese Communists did what no foreign power could probably ever do—they overwhelmed the existing government of China, gained favor with the majority of the people, and then proceeded to build a new government for all of China. No longer would Chinese strength be a rope of sand.

Mao Tse-tung quickly consolidated his position and that of the revolutionary regime. The People's Republic of China was formed at Peking on 1 October, 1949. Through the use of coercive measures, but more important, through a large measure of popular support, the new regime was able to unify the country more completely than any other power had done since the height of the Manchu Dynasty which had lasted from 1640 to 1840.

It is not surprising that the regime was aggressive, and exhibited feelings of hatred and contempt toward the West. During the centuries prior to 1840, the

Chinese kept to themselves in their own land, and considered foreigners to be inferior and barbaric. This is important to understanding the aggressive position of China. China had suffered humiliation from 1840 until 1950. Before the western nations had gained a foothold in China, Chinese expected that the foreigner would first pay tribute, and then do his business.

It is strange that a doctrine from a man like Marx could be adapted to a land with a million peasants. Marx thought primarily in terms of the urban masses and industrial workers. However, he had an apt pupil in Lenin, who could adapt the theories to Russia, with millions of peasants only a half-century removed from serfdom. Mao had a good leader to follow. What Lenin did in Russia, Mao could do in China. Sun Yat-sen had been a disciple of Lenin to a degree, but he denied the need for class struggle. In comparison with the rigid militancy of Mao, Sun was mild.

Mao turned the tenets of Marxism inside out and upside-down. He based his movement on the peasant. Rather than think of the international revolutionary aspects, he concentrated on using his forces to create a strong China. The International World Revolution was not forgotten. It would come later, and would be pure, not corrupted by revisionism. In 1926, Mao first promulgated his revised ideas of Communism. About a decade later, he emphasized the national character of his movement. He wanted to create a Chinese Marxism, and did. This became the thought of Comrade Mao.

Stalin himself felt more affinity for Sun Yat-sen and the Kuomintang Party, believing it would best serve Russia's interests. Stalin probably feared Mao and his brand of Chinese Marxism. Sun Yat-sen's young aide, Chiang Kai-shek, forged strong armies with Russian aid, and by 1927, had conquered much of China from the regional war lords. Now he turned on his allies and outwitted Stalin. The Chinese Communist movement had concentrated western-style on the cities. It had no solid basis among the peasantry. Chiang was ruthless in his suppression of Chinese Communists from 1927-1930. Mao then gathered his people and climbed the slopes of Ching Kan Shen, his first stronghold. Chinese Communism, based on the proletariat, had failed. Now Mao with his shrewd upside-down Marxism would base his Communism on the peasant and the earth.

Mao gave the peasants what they wanted—revenge against the landlord. He was an intellectual warrior, and carried on a brilliant guerrilla campaign against the Kuomintang. In his celebrated long march to the north in 1934-35, he won admiration from all sides. During the military campaigns of this period, Mao stands out, like General Lee, as a brilliant general with an elite corps, against an adversary who outnumbered him. Time and again, he was as successful as Lee in dividing and conquering the enemy, and Chiang was no Grant.

When we look back to the 1949 era and to prevalent attitudes in the United States, it does not seem possible that we could have so readily blamed General

Marshall, the China Desk in the State Department, and the "pinks" in governmen
for having sold Chiang down the river. China was lost, so it was said, because we
did not support the Nationalist Government properly.

Considering China on the flank of Soviet Russia, with an impoverished, ex
ploited peasantry, the triumph of Communism was practically inevitable.

Professor Tang, in *Communist China Today*, has quoted Chairman Mao a
saying that 1919 was the turning point in the Chinese Revolution. In that year, i
was transformed from a bourgeois-type to a new proletarian-type revolution.[3] Thi
period could also be called the turning point in Chinese-American relations. Durin
the year 1915, a strong reaction set in among the Chinese intellectuals at th
University of Peking. Instead of looking East to the old Chinese tradition, the
looked to the West and planned to follow the Japanese example. This was the wa
to obtain new principles and infuse new life into decadent Chinese institutions an
to revitalize ideas. Feudalism in the Confucian tradition had held China back. Nov
Western methods would be tried. An early leader in this movement in 1915 wa
Ch'en Tu-Hsio, a professor at the University of Peking. The European Armistice o
1918 brought hope to this scholar and his associates. Particularly important wa
President Wilson and his Fourteen Points. Soon the Germans would be out o
China. The stage had been set for a mighty shock. Within six months, China ha
suffered a defeat at the Peace Table. On 4 May, 1919, the news reached Peking
There was an immediate bitter reaction. Secret agreements had prevailed at Ver
sailles. German rights in Shangtung Province were handed over to Japan. Th
Chinese delegation had demanded that foreign privileges in China be abrogated
They were not. We are still reaping the whirlwind in bitter harvest.

China had been sold out to Japan. Later, during the 1930's, America deplore
Japanese Imperialism in China, but continued to sell Japan scrap metal. From
1926 on, the United States gave tacit support to Chiang. The aid was wasted, but i
continued. American equipment was well used by the People's Army. Even Gen
eral Stilwell was unable to convince the government that aid to Nationalist Chin
was not going to stem the tide of Chinese Communism. We backed the losing sid
in the Chinese Civil War.

FOOTNOTES

[1] Morison, Samuel Eliot, *The Maritime History of Massachusetts (1783-1860)* Sentr
Edition (Boston: Houghton Mifflin Company, 1961) p. 44.

[2] *Ibid.*, p. 45.

[3] Tang, Peter S. H., *Communist China Today*, Second Ed., Research Institute on th
Sino-Soviet Bloc, Washington, D.C., 1961, p. 30.

CHAPTER IV

CHINA, THE UNITED STATES, AND THE UNITED NATIONS

Many Americans believe that the United Nations had its start either at the 1945 San Francisco Conference, or in President Roosevelt's White House study. The Russians consider that the first practical step toward the creation of a new international organization was taken in Moscow. "Moscow became the birthplace of the United Nations" according to S. B. Krylov, a Soviet scientist who participated in the 1943 Three-Power Foreign Ministers' Conference held in Moscow. "It was in Moscow that the declaration on establishing an international organization for security was signed."[1]

The British feel differently. On 12 June, 1941, at the most desperate period of Britain's struggle against Nazism, representatives of the countries at war with Nazi Germany, and of nine governments in exile, met at St. James Palace and approved the London Declaration.[2] At that time, Soviet Russia and Nazi Germany were trading with each other.

On 10 January, 1941, Russia and Nazi Germany had signed a trade deal to run until 1 August, 1942. The Third Reich was to receive from the Soviet Union food, grains, industrial raw materials, and oil products in exchange for industrial equipment. Pravda editorials stated that Russia would follow an independent policy in making commercial treaties with other nations whether they were at peace or war. Izvestia said that economic relations between the U.S.S.R. and Germany would form a most effective means of strengthening peace and friendship.[3]

On 12 June, 1941, representatives of fifteen Dominion and Allied governments adopted a resolution to fight against German aggression until victory. On this same day, it was reported in Stockholm that the Germans were massing troops on the Russian border and demanding concessions in the Ukraine and Caucasus. Ten days later, Germany declared war on Russia. The Russians had not heeded the warnings of British Intelligence.

The London Declaration, issued while Germany and Russia were still allies, announced the intention of free peoples to establish a world in which all would enjoy economic and social security. Two weeks after the London Declaration, diplomats in Ankara reported that Franz von Papen, the German Ambassador to Turkey, offered peace to Britain the day Germany invaded Russia. It was reported that Germany wanted Britain to join in a coalition against the Soviet Union. Sir Hughe Knatchbull-Hugessen, British Ambassador to Turkey, referred Mr. Papen to

Churchill's speech of 22 June, 1941, in which the Prime Minister pledged immediate and full aid to Russia.

On 14 August, 1941, Roosevelt and Churchill met at sea and issued a joint declaration, known as the Atlantic Charter. President Roosevelt and Prime Minister Churchill sent a joint message to Premier Stalin after issuing the Atlantic Charter Communiqué. The message urged a conference in Moscow to discuss apportioning joint resources to defeat Hitlerism. Secretary of State Hull hoped that all civilized nations, including Russia, would accept the Roosevelt-Churchill program. Article Eight, of the Atlantic Charter, called for a world peace organization. The United Nations' Declaration of 1942, issued from President Roosevelt's White House study, was based on the purposes and principles of the London Declaration and the Atlantic Charter.[4]

There is substantial difference of opinion on responsibility for the founding of the United Nations. However, all nations agree on several concepts. One of these is universality. The United Nations was to be open to all states on the principle of sovereign equality.

In the Moscow Declaration of 1 November, 1943, the foreign Ministers of the United Kingdom, the Union of Soviet Socialist Republics, the United States, and the Chinese Ambassador in Moscow reaffirmed the unity of their countries in the conduct of the war. They pledged to remain united after the war in a general international organization based on the principle of the sovereign equality of peace-loving states. The body was to be open to membership by all states, large or small. The Moscow Declaration called for an organization which, in its broad outlines, was the League of Nations under a new name. The Preamble of the Charter was based on a draft prepared by Field Marshal Smuts, at London Commonwealth Meetings in 1945. Field Marshal Smuts repeated the distinguished role he had played twenty-six years before, during the drafting of the League Covenant.[5]

During the late 1930's, while Congress was passing the successive neutrality acts, the majority of League members declared they no longer considered binding the obligations of the Covenant. During the League's best years its agencies continued to meet and perform useful tasks. Main international problems, however, were dealt with outside Geneva. Big power diplomacy did not work.

During a swift succession of crises—the Spanish Civil War; Japan's invasion of China; and the annexation of Austria, Czechoslovakia, and Albania—references to the League were either mere formalities, or omitted.

When World War II broke out in September of 1939, no appeal of any sort was made to Geneva. In December, 1939, Finland did appeal for help against Russian aggression. The Assembly excluded Russia from the League. It did organize such help for Finland as it could. Nothing else was done. During the war, there were no further meetings of the Council or Assembly. The League's political activity was at an end. Thanks to Canadian and American hospitality, the economic and social work of the League was continued on a limited scale.

Churchill and Roosevelt, in their plan for a future international organization, rejected any idea of reviving the Covenant. It had the stigma of defeat. The Covenant was still nominally in force when the United Nations began to function in October, 1945.

Shortly after Pearl Harbor, the United Nations Declaration was signed by President Roosevelt, T. V. Soong, Foreign Minister, representing China, M. Litvinov, the Soviet Ambassador the United States, and Winston Churchill. The Declaration by itself did not win battles, but it enumerated the member nations, and what they stood for. The majestic document was signed in President Roosevelt's study. It was left to the State Department to collect the signatures of the remaining twenty-two nations.[6]

President Roosevelt dealt with Churchill as a friend, with de Gaulle as a cross to bear, with Stalin as an ally and with Chiang Kai-shek as the leader of a nation with five hundred million people. This nation, by virtue of its size, population and potential importance in Asian affairs had to become one of the founding members of the United Nations with a permanent seat on the Security Council. Roosevelt, the aristocrat of democracy, had a great respect for the Chinese population. He insisted on treating China as a great power, when its actual power was small. The title of "United Nations" was substituted by the President for "Associated Powers." Churchill thought this to be a great improvement. He showed his friend the lines from Byron's *Childe Harold*.[7]

"Here, where the sword United Nations drew,
    Our countrymen were warring on that day!
And this is much—and all—which will not pass away."

Now the President was the chief propagandist for the Allies. He proclaimed the Four Freedoms. The battle was not only one of armies and navies, but of ideas and symbols as well.[8] Hitler interpreted the war to his people as a struggle of the masses against the plutocratic nations of the world. The President of the United States had a constituency of three-quarters of the world. He affirmed freedom as the supreme symbol of the cause for which the Allies fought. As Hitler sought to divest this symbol of any meaning except liberty to exploit the masses, Roosevelt sought to strengthen the idea of freedom as a positive idea—as freedom to gain peace and security after the war. Roosevelt insisted on freedom and insisted on proper Chinese participation. He felt that there could be no security with five hundred million Chinese unrepresented. Roosevelt also exerted his utmost efforts to persuade Litvinov, the Soviet ambassador, to accept the phrase "religious freedom." Roosevelt invited Litvinov to a private lunch with Churchill. A lecture was delivered to Litvinov about his soul and the dangers of hellfire—a lecture just like Headmaster Peabody would have given at Groton. Churchill was so impressed that he offered to recommend Roosevelt for the position of Archbishop of Canterbury, if he should lose the next presidential election. Litvinov reported the issue about "religious freedom" in evident fear and trembling to Stalin, who accepted it as a matter of course.[9] Stalin did not care about religious freedom, but he gave the opposite impression for the sake of expediency.

Churchill and Roosevelt, great partners in the Grand Alliance, were poles apart on China. Roosevelt might be dreaming about future populations, but Churchill and Stalin were concerned with present power. The President wanted Churchill to meet Madame Chiang Kai-shek in the White House in May, 1942. Madame Chiang was in New York and was invited by Roosevelt for a visit with Churchill. The Madame declined with some hauteur, thinking that Churchill should make a pilgrimage to New York to see her.[10] Churchill, in his desire to preserve unity in the Grand Alliance, offered to go halfway. Perhaps they could have met at Independence Hall, or at Glassboro. The offer was considered facetious, and Churchill never had the pleasure and advantage of meeting the lady until the Cairo Conference. This was not an auspicious foundation for Chiang Kai-shek's later participation in that Conference.

During the summer of 1942, fuel was added to the fire of Churchill's dislike for Chiang. Just before the great North African Battle at El Alamein, Churchill had visited Moscow and Cairo. While he was away from London, the Congress Party in India committed themselves to an aggressive policy of sabotage, riots and disorder. The Viceroy's Council, subsequently, ordered the arrest of Gandhi, Nehru, and the principal Congress Party members. Generalissimo Chiang Kai-shek sent voluminous protests to the President. Churchill resented this intervention bitterly.[11] He also resented Roosevelt's intrusion in Indian affairs. In a memorandum to his Foreign Secretary, Churchill said that he did not consider China to be a great power.[12] The minds of Churchill and Roosevelt never met on the China issue and England and America have not had a unified China policy since.

In 1943, Churchill, Roosevelt, and Chiang Kai-shek met at Cairo. Formosa was promised to Chiang, and he was sent home. At Teheran, Stalin met with Roosevelt and Churchill. Roosevelt later bragged about his ability to negotiate with Stalin. He deliberately baited Churchill about his Britishness, cigars and habits.[13] Churchill was no man to bait, and no friend of Chiang. Churchill stood by while the hard series of compromises was hammered out in January of 1945. In the Far East, Stalin was granted the Kurile Islands, the southern part of Sakhalin, and extensive spheres of influence in North China.[14] The granite-hard son of serfs, schooled in blood and violence, was way ahead of his adversaries. Churchill was aware of the realities, but he did not have the continental land power to give strength to his strategy.

In the spring of 1946, the Assembly of the League met at Geneva for the last time. The powers and functions entrusted to the League by many treaties were transferred to the new organization. On 19 April, 1946, the League formally ended. The United Nations inherited its material possessions, including the *Palais des Nations*.

The United Nations was also to inherit one of the major problems of the League, i.e. non-participation by all the great powers. A generation ago, the United States Senate failed to ratify the League Covenant and the action was decisive for the future of the League. The possibility of collective security, as embodied in the Covenant, was precluded. It had been expected that certain complete economic boycott would make even the most aggressive government prefer to settle its disputes by negotiations, rather than by armed attack. The knowledge that the world's greatest economic power would stand aside from sanctions robbed the Covenant of its main deterrent for would-be aggressors. Members' confidence in the League had been destroyed by United States' failure to become a member.

The League had been the dream of an American president, who wanted peace without victory. The League failed, because it did not have universal membership. Now, years later, the United Nations does not have universal membership. Although an American president was the first Western statesman to insist upon great power status for a non-Western state, the people of America have prevented full participation in the United Nations by that non-Western power, i.e. China.

The transfer of power and property to the United Nations from the League, in 1946, was a melancholy occasion for those who believed in the principles of the Covenant. The provisions of the Charter were drafted in an attempt to rectify the faults of the Covenant. However, it remained true that in its purposes and principles, its institutions and its methods, the institution created by the Charter followed the precedents of the institution which had failed. Lack of universality might make the United Nations fail, also.

The United Nations had been in existence for five years before the People of China were internationally disenfranchised. A successful revolution took place in China. The Republic of China, a founding member of the United Nations, was defeated in a civil war. That government moved to the Island of Formosa in 1949. It became the effective government of an island with a population of thirteen million. A new government on mainland China was established in Peking. This government exercised effective control over 500 million people. The Republic of China on Formosa pretended to govern mainland-China from Formosa. But it did not exercise effective control over China proper. Public opinion in the United States would not allow the United States government to recognize these basic facts in the case of China.

Field Marshal J. C. Smuts' idea that an international organization must be not only a diplomatic defense against war, but also a great civilizing influence throughout the political system, was not realized in the League. It is yet to be realized in the United Nations.

After World War II, and particularly after the Korean War, the United States acted alone in attempts to isolate China. Britain, as a trading island nation, practically recognized the facts of Chinese power.

At age 56, Mao proclaimed the People's Republic of China. The opening session of the People's Political Consultative Conference was held in Peking, on 21 September, 1949. The new government made no immediate bid for world recognition. It was expected to do so. It was also expected to challenge the United Nations to let it take over China's representation from Nationalist delegates.

On 15 November, 1949, the Chinese Communist regime made its first bid for U.N. recognition. Peking radioed a message to Lake Success declaring that the Nationalist delegation, led by T.F. Tsiang, had no right to speak for the Chinese people. The United States balked at recognition, because U.S. Consul General, Angus Ward, was under arrest in Mukden.

Angus Ward and four members of his staff were freed on 25 November. A Mukden court had convicted them of beating a former servant. They were given a three-to-six-month jail sentence, which was changed to deportation. On 23 November, 1949, Russia informed the U.N. General Assembly that it no longer recognized the Nationalists' right to represent China in the United Nations.

On 1 January, 1950, the United States decided against using American forces to defend Formosa. The U.S. Joint Chiefs and Secretary Acheson had argued successfully against American defense of Formosa on these grounds:

1) Island not vital to U.S. security.
2) Occupation might throw United States into war with Chinese Communists and Russia.
3) Chiang's Nationalists could not be trusted to make good use of U.S. aid, and, besides, they were hated by the Formosans.
4) U.S. occupation of the island would have bad political effects in Southeast Asia. Formosa was a Chinese question to be settled by the Chinese.

The State Department disclosed on 3 January, 1950, that the Chinese Nationalists had requested military assistance to defend Formosa. On 5 January, President Truman issued a statement making it clear that the United States would provide no such aid. It was also made clear that the United States had no predatory designs on Formosa or other Chinese territory. The United States would pursue no course of action which might involve it in the China conflict. Moscow may have seen this as a green light to go into South Korea. It has never been shown that China was involved in the original Korean aggression.

In December, 1949, President Truman declared that the United States would not interfere further in the Chinese Civil War.[15] The Chinese undoubtedly anticipated a quick North Korean victory six months later when South Korea was attacked. The Chinese also felt that they would soon be able to invade and conquer Taiwan. President Truman acted quickly to resist aggression in Korea. We forget that he was fighting Russian Imperialism. The inspiration for aggression in Korea had come from Moscow, not Peking. The 38th Parallel, as a dividing line in Korea, was never the subject of international discussion before 1950. The United States proposed it as a practicable solution when the sudden collapse of Japan created a vacuum in Korea. The State Department urged that in all Korea the surrender of Japanese forces should be taken by Americans. There was no way, however, to get our troops into the northern part of the country without sacrificing the security of our initial landings in Japan. The Russians went into North Korea. Stalin had concurred in the idea of a joint trusteeship. It was expected that the division of the country would be solely for the purpose of accepting the Japanese surrender. The Russians, however, immediately began to treat the 38th Parallel as a permanent dividing line. A joint commission working on the problem with the Russians adjourned *sine die* on 8 May, 1946, without having solved the problem.[16]

The United States knew that the Russians had built up a "People's Army" in North Korea. In the spring of 1948, President Truman advised the National Security Council that the United States would extend to the Republic of Korea assistance to prevent a breakdown of that infant nation.[17]

FOOTNOTES

[1] Grigory Morozov and Evgeny Pehelintsev, *The United Nations–Twenty Years of Failures and Successes* (Moscow: Novosti Press Publishing House, 1965) p. 10.

[2] British Information Services, *Britain and the United Nations* (London: Reference Division, Central Office of Information, 1964) p. 3.

[3] Facts on File, Vol. I, 1941, p. 85.

[4] British Information Services, *op. cit.*, p. 3.

[5] *Ibid.*, p. 4.

[6] Churchill, Winston S., *The Grand Alliance* (Boston: Houghton Mifflin Company, 1951) p. 683.

[7] *Ibid.*, p. 683.

[8] Burns, James MacGregor, *Roosevelt, The Lion and the Fox* (New York: Harcourt, Brace & World, Inc., 1956) p. 465.

[9] Churchill, *op. cit.*, p. 683.

[10] Churchill, Winston S., *The Hinge of Fate* (Boston: Houghton Mifflin Company, 1951) p. 797.

[11] *Ibid.*, p. 507.

[12] *Ibid.*, p. 562.

[13] Burns, *op. cit.*, p. 465.

[14] *Ibid.*, p. 469.

[15] Whiting, Allan S., *China Crosses the Yalu*, The Rand Corporation (New York: The MacMillan Company, 1960) p. 49.

[16] Truman, Harry S., Memoirs, Vol. II, *Years of Trial and Hope, 1946-1952* (New York: Doubleday & Company, Inc., 1956) p. 320.

[17] *Ibid.*, p. 328.

CHAPTER V

POST-KOREAN WAR CHINESE-AMERICAN RELATIONS

In June of 1950 there was no doubt that the Republic of Korea needed help at once if it was not to be overrun. A Communist success in Korea would put Red troops and planes within easy striking distance of Japan. What developed in Korea seemed to President Truman to be a repetition of what had happened in Berlin. The Russians were probing for weaknesses in our armor. On 27 June, 1950, President Truman directed the Secretary of Defense to call General MacArthur on the scrambler phone and give him instructions in person. General MacArthur was ordered to:

1) Use air and naval forces to support the Republic of Korea, but only south of the 38th Parallel.

2) Dispatch the Seventh Fleet to the Formosa Strait to prevent attacks by the Communists on Formosa, as well as forays by Chiang Kai-shek against the mainland. This last instruction was given to avoid reprisals by the Chinese Communists that might enlarge the area of conflict.[1]

After war had broken out in Korea, the United States was once again involved with force in the Straits of Formosa. In January, 1950, we decided not to interfere further in the Chinese Civil War. Then, in June, 1950, to counter Russian Imperialism, the Seventh Fleet was ordered to patrol waters off the Chinese Coast. The United States Fleet was also used to prevent attacks by Chiang on mainland-China. President Truman wanted to confine the conflict to Korea.

In 1950, a General Assembly study committee was formed to study the China question. This committee did not make satisfactory recommendations to the General Assembly. The report was "noted" and filed. Attempts to refer the issue to the new Assembly were dropped. The 1966 Italian Study Committee proposal showed little forward movement since the 1950 Canadian Study Committee proposal. According to the Canadians, a new study committee would have to be guided by a specific mandate from the General Assembly in its attempts to explore the elements of an equitable solution. Without such a directive, the study committee would be just wasting time.[2] The Chinese on Formosa and in Peking agreed only that there was one China, but each government insisted it was the legitimate government of China. Discussion of two Chinas would never succeed, because both principals adamantly held that there was only one China.

Between 1951 and 1961 there was no substantive discussion of Chinese representation in the General Assembly. During these years, the United States proposed, at the beginning of each session, to postpone consideration of the Chinese representation question for the duration of that session. Each year, the United States' proposal was adopted; at first, by a large majority, and then, by slowly declining majorities. By 1960, the margin voting for postponement had become slim: 42 in favor, 34 against, and 22 abstentions. For a decade the matter was considered by the Assembly's Steering Committee, but action was deferred. The Credentials Committee during these years submitted reports to the General Assembly which supported the Chinese Nationalists. The General Assembly approved these reports, and further discussions were not permitted. There was constant discussion of the question, but no debate as such in the General Assembly.

The United States has used various delaying tactics, but not the veto. On 12 May, 1944, Secretary of State, Cordell Hull, made a two-hour appearance before the Senate Committee on Foreign Relations. Eight senators had just read the draft for the United Nations Organization. One of the senators thought it would be a serious defect to let any one of the major nations kill a proposal by veto.

Cordell Hull replied: "The veto power is in the document primarily on account of the United States. It is a necessary safeguard in dealing with a new and untried world arrangement." Later, Hull went on to say that the United States government could not move any faster than an alert public opinion would allow it to move.[3]

The veto has been used by all permanent members of the Security Council. The United States has used it once. Only the Soviet Union has used the veto frequently. Essentially, the veto is a reminder of the facts of life, of the realities of power politics.

The United States had let it be known occasionally before 1970 that it might use the veto. These veto threats have been sufficient to prevent American representatives from having to cast a veto, except in the recent Rhodesia vote. In 1950, the United States said that it would veto any candidate to replace Trygve Lie as Secretary General.[4] Russia had vetoed Lie on 12 October, 1950. The United States stated that it would block each one of the four possible successors acceptable to Russia. Lie wanted Red China to have a United Nations seat, but Russia was opposed to Lie because of United Nations action in Korea.[5]

After the Korean Armistice in 1953, Mr. Dulles told Mr. Rhee, of South Korea, that the United States did not intend to buy the unity of Korea at the price of a United Nations seat for Communist China. He made no promise that the United States would use its veto, but indicated that, in view of Soviet veto policy, the United States would feel free to do so.

On 3 March, 1950, in an advisory opinion, the International Court of Justice in The Hague decided 12-2 that the U.N. Charter did not permit the General Assembly to admit to U.N. membership applicants vetoed or otherwise rejected by the Security Council. This decision had been requested by the Assembly in 1949. The Court decision upheld the views of Russia and the U.S.A.

Trygve Lie, a short time later, implied that the Communists should be admitted as Chinese U.N. representatives. Dr. Tsiang, the Chinese Nationalist delegate, said that Lie, by this proposal, undermined public confidence in his impartiality. Acheson said that the United States would vote against Red China, but would not use the veto.

In May of 1950, Mr. Acheson said again that the United States would not veto admission of Red China to the United Nations. This statement was made in an address to a Joint Session of Congress. It was reported that all members applauded Acheson at the conclusion of his remarks except Senator Joseph R. McCarthy, who called Acheson the 'Red Dean' of Washington. It is interesting to note in Mr. Acheson's memoirs that his villain was not so much Senator Joseph McCarthy, but fellow Yale man Robert A. Taft.

Mr. Lie contended that it should be United Nations policy to deal with whatever government exercises effective authority. Early in June, 1950, Lie visited Washington, Moscow, Paris, and London. He asked the Big Four to end their deadlock on admitting Communist China to the United Nations. In a letter to all 59 members, Lie put forth a ten-point, twenty-year program for achieving peace through the United Nations. He pleaded that no progress could be made through the United Nations on major cold-war issues until the Soviet bloc walkouts on Chinese representation were settled. It was generally understood that Lie wanted the West to accept Communist representation of China as a permanent Security Council member. Acheson replied that the United States would not be coerced by Russian boycott pressure. Russia then launched its June, 1950, attack, using the puppet North Korean forces.

In mid-July, Stalin offered a deal on China. If the Communists were given China's seat on the Security Council, then Russia would return to the Council and help negotiate peace in Korea. It was too late. Stalin's bluff had been called by Truman. Acheson replied through Nehru that the United States would not be coerced and agree under duress to admit China.

In December of 1950, Truman and Attlee would not allow their difference over Red Chinese U.N. membership to upset the basic Anglo-United States Alliance. Their joint communiqué mentioned the difference. It implied that overwhelming popular opinion in the United States against Red China ruled out a compromise. It was United States policy to oppose Red China's admission to the United Nations, but not to veto it in Security Council. Acheson supposedly reported to a Foreign Affairs Committee of Congress that the veto could be used to bar a country from the United Nations, but not to decide which faction of a country should be admitted. This interpretation of the veto use was based on the March 1950 Hague ruling on the use of the veto.

In May, 1951, Acheson again said that China was a United Nations member. The question of which faction should represent China was not vetoable under the United Nations rules.

When President Truman met General MacArthur at Wake Island, on 15 October, 1950, the General assured the President that the Chinese Communists would not attack in Korea.[6] He then apologized for his Formosa statement to the Veterans of Foreign Wars. If Chou En-lai had known of this apology, perhaps Communist China would not have seen the thrust over the 38th Parallel as a threat to Manchuria. Upon returning to San Francisco, President Truman said that he had had a good talk with General MacArthur. North Korean aggression was simply Colonialism—Soviet-style. The President concluded his remarks by saying that we were not a militaristic nation. We had no desire for conquest or military glory. No country in the world which really wanted peace had any reason to fear the United States of America—but China did fear General MacArthur.

Serious problems had been building up between MacArthur and Truman ever since mid-summer, 1950. On 31 July, 1950, General MacArthur had made a trip to Formosa. This trip had raised much speculation in the world press. Chiang Kai-shek's aides let it be known that the Far East commander was in fullest agreement with Chiang on a course of action to take. The implication was that MacArthur rejected President Truman's policy of neutralizing Formosa, and that he favored a more aggressive path. President Truman asked Averell Harriman to explain Administration policy to MacArthur. President Truman was reassured after MacArthur told Harriman that he would accept official policy as a good soldier. It was assumed that this would be the last of the Formosa discussion. It was not.[7]

On 28 August, 1950, General MacArthur sent a statement to the Commander-in-Chief of the Veterans of Foreign Wars. MacArthur called for a military policy of aggression based on Formosa's position. Earlier United States action in placing the Seventh Fleet in the Formosa Straits was meant only to reduce the area of conflict in the Far East. MacArthur's statement made it appear that Formosa had been placed within the American orbit. General MacArthur's message contradicted announced American political policy.[8] Serious consideration was given to removing General MacArthur. General MacArthur was, instead, ordered to withdraw the statement. He did so at once.

Chinese prisoners captured on 31 October, 1950, stated that their units had crossed the Yalu on 16 October, 1950. This was only one day after General MacArthur had assured President Truman, on Wake Island, that if any Chinese were to enter Korea, they would face certain disaster. General MacArthur had wanted to make a dramatic announcement on 1 October, 1950, on the occasion of crossing the 38th Parallel. The Joint Chiefs of Staff stopped only the dramatic announcement. On 3 October, 1950, the State Department received a number of messages, threatening that the Chinese Communists were on the verge of entering the Korean conflict. These messages were at once transmitted to General Mac-Arthur. At Wake Island, the General repeated that the Korean conflict was won, and that there was little possibility of the Chinese Communists becoming involved.

The Joint Chiefs of Staff had informed MacArthur that in his advance he should not place non-Korean elements near the Manchurian and Soviet borders. However, in his orders, the General provided for the drive to the north to be spearheaded by American units. The Joint Chiefs were concerned, and asked MacArthur the reasons for this change. MacArthur replied that he did not have much confidence in the Koreans and wanted the drive to be spearheaded by experienced American commanders.[9]

While MacArthur's forces were moving north, there was speculation about the likelihood of the Chinese Communists taking some action in North Korea. On 20 October, 1950, the C.I.A. delivered a memorandum to President Truman which stated that the Chinese Communists would move in far enough to guard the Suiho Electric Plant and other generating stations along the Yalu. The State Department wanted to publicly announce that these installations would not be touched. The Joint Chiefs replied that this, militarily, would be unwise. On 31 October, we obtained evidence that the Chinese had already made their move into North Korea. It is doubtful that any statement regarding the power houses would have made any difference.[10]

With their entry into the Korean War, the Chinese Communists had staked their forces and their prestige in Asia. President Truman did not want our action in Korea to become a general war. All-out military action against China had to be avoided, because it was a gigantic booby trap. The C.I.A.'s estimate of the situation was that the Russians themselves were not willing to go to war. But they want to involve us heavily in Asia to give them a free hand in Europe.

President Truman blamed MacArthur only for the manner in which he excused his failure. MacArthur publicized the view that the only reason for his troubles was the order from Washington to limit the hostilities to Korea. He said on occasion that, if only his advice had been followed, all would have been well in Korea. If his advice had been followed, and we had bombed Manchurian bases, then we would have been openly at war with Red China, and, not improbably, with Russia. World War III might have started in Korea.[11]

At a press conference on 30 November, 1950, President Truman stated that he hoped the Chinese people would not continue to be deceived into serving the ends of Russian colonial policy in Asia. The massive counterblow by which the Chinese halted MacArthur's offensive was, perhaps, more of a shock in Europe than it was at home. There were open predictions that we would disregard the United Nations and plunge into general war with China. The atomic bomb was mentioned by

President Truman in a press conference and touched off a furor in Britain. Prime Minister Attlee flew to Washington for urgent conferences with President Truman. At these conferences, Secretary Acheson pointed out that the central enemy was the Soviet Union, not China. What price would the Chinese Communists demand in negotiations? No one knew the answer. Prime Minister Attlee was told what had transpired at Wake Island. Truman had told MacArthur to avoid provoking the Chinese in Manchuria. Attlee pointed out that he thought the Chinese Communists were ripe for "Titoism." China was not completely in Russian hands. The Russians and Chinese were natural enemies in the Far East.[12]

Prime Minister Attlee felt that China should have a seat in the United Nations. The British did not pretend that the "nasty fellow" on the other side was not there. Once the Chinese Communists were in the United Nations, we could use the principles of the Charter as arguments in dealing with them. President Truman said that we would face terrible divisions among our people if the Chinese Communists were admitted to the U.N. after they had committed aggression in Korea. Dean Rusk, then our Assistant Secretary of State in charge of Far Eastern affairs, said there was no reason for us to prove our good will by agreeing to seat Chinese Communists in the U.N. in order to get a settlement. The question of Red China's admission to the United Nations was considered a sort of bribe to stop the Korean War. Truman finally said "No." The American people would never stand for it. In the long run, he felt that the Chinese would find that their real friends were not in Moscow and Siberia, but in London and Washington.[13]

President Truman never believed that MacArthur did not realize that the "introduction of Chinese Nationalist forces into South China" would be an act of war. In December of 1950, MacArthur advocated this policy to General Collins in secret talks. Enough was known of MacArthur's views among the press to give the American public the impression that he offered the only sure way to victory in Korea. General MacArthur was ready to risk a general war. President Truman was not.[14]

On 24 March, 1951, MacArthur issued a statement implying that there might be a shift in United Nations policy. There might be a departure from the policy of containment in Korea. General MacArthur emphasized that an expansion of our military operations to China's coastal areas would hasten the military collapse of Red China. This was a call to unleash Chiang. By this act, MacArthur left Truman no choice. The President could no longer tolerate the General's insubordination. MacArthur had openly defied the policy of his Commander in Chief, the President of the United States.[13]

MacArthur talked as if he knew all the answers. When it turned out that this was not so, he let the world know that he would have won if we had let him have his way. General MacArthur had recommended that we accept Chiang's offer to use thirty-three thousand Chinese Nationalists troops in Korea. He believed the

Korean War had become a war against Communist China. President Truman said that he should have relieved General MacArthur in November of 1950 when the General advocated using Nationalist Chinese aid, contrary to government policy.[16] MacArthur was not relieved until 11 April, 1951.

The Truman Administration's opposition to Red Chinese participation in the United Nations is interwoven with the Truman-MacArthur controversy. Before the Korean War, it appeared that the United States would eventually accept the facts of the Chinese Civil War.

Secretary of State Acheson's stand on China was clear and straightforward from the time he took office until 25 June, 1950, when it was changed by war in Korea. Perhaps the most striking phenomenon of Acheson's tenure in office was the extraordinary disparity between what he accomplished in office and the opinion in which he was held by a large number of his countrymen.[17] Because Mr. Acheson would not turn his back on an old friend, Alger Hiss, he was vilified. It would seem as if he had recommended Hiss for new, top-secret security clearance, rather than having simply stated that he would not turn his back on Hiss. After General MacArthur was relieved, there was a clamor for President Truman to fire Dean Acheson. Some senators thought that this would promote the national interest. Truman believed that history would consider Dean Acheson a truly great Secretary of State. The President said that if Communism were to prevail in the world, the first person to be shot by the enemies of liberty and Christianity would have been Mr. Acheson. Communism, not the United States, would have been served by losing him.[18]

In his year-end review of 1950, Secretary of State Acheson stated that the United States would not compromise, by appeasement, the principles by which free men live. He announced that we would not reward Communist aggression. The Politburo was castigated for sanctimoniously professing peace which, it was felt, merely camouflaged its naked imperialist aims.[19]

In December, 1950, when Truman met Attlee aboard the *Williamsburg*, General Marshall stated that he knew they were all agreed on staying out of a general war with China, and that was was a real threat. However, we were dealing with a government with whom it was impossible to negotiate. It would be very dangerous to go into negotiations at a time, and in a way, that would only reveal our weakness.[20]

We could not afford to let Formosa go. It was not strategically important in our hands; it would be disastrously important if held by an enemy. General Marshall had no immediate answer to the problem, except to maintain our position and use the time to gather strength on all fronts.

President Truman interjected history of the Cairo Declaration with regard to Formosa. The declaration had been framed when Japan was the Pacific enemy. Our objective then had been to establish a power in the Pacific friendly to the

United States. Now the situation was reversed. The nation we had hoped to establish—China—had not only fallen into unfriendly hands, but was viciously hostile to the United States.[21]

During this period, the big lie technique of Senator McCarthy was being perfected. Mr. Acheson appeared before the Senate Foreign Relations Committee, regarding the MacArthur ouster, during the first week of June, 1951. He denied that he ever stood for appeasing the Communists in China or anywhere else. Acheson upheld MacArthur's removal from command although he had feared the furor it would cause. Senator Joseph McCarthy, a spectator at the hearings, fed questions to G.O.P. Committeemen. Acheson denied that he was even acquainted with Owen Lattimore, whom Senator McCarthy had charged was a pro-Soviet influence on United States-China policy. Acheson defended a memo sent out in December, 1949, in which he told United States diplomats to prepare public opinion for Communist capture of Formosa. Acheson finally stated that Formosa's future should be decided by the United Nations. He hoped that the United Nations would not vote to admit Peking to membership. Acheson also said that the United States could not prevent discussion of the question.[22] In his review of the year 1951, Acheson said that in Korea we had contended against aggression with firm resolution and sensible restraint. These were two qualities needed for the long pull ahead. The United States would have to remain on guard against a renewal of Communist treachery.[23]

Until after the 1952 election, the United States strategy in the United Nations regarding the Chinese membership was to fight a delaying action. The United States wanted to keep Red China out while the war lasted. The Chinese could not come in as a bribe to end the war. The general attitude was to settle the Korean War and then take another look at the situation.

At a news conference on 16 May, 1951, Secretary Acheson was asked about General Marshall's view that the United States should veto Chinese Communist membership in the U.N. Acheson replied that it would louse up (Acheson's phrase) the issue to regard it as something to be vetoed. China was already a member. The question of which Chinese faction should represent China in the UN was not vetoable under U.N. rules. Acheson believed that General Marshall had been misunderstood. The United States' procedure was to persuade a majority of United Nations members to oppose giving China's seat to the Communists. When asked about resigning, Acheson said that he had "enlisted for the duration." He would not resign until Mr. Truman wanted him to.[24]

In the United Nations, the 1950 Assembly Session formally ended on 5 November, 1951. On its last day, it "noted" a recent Committee report on the disagreement over Chinese representation. It rejected 20-11 (11 abstentions) a Soviet resolution that the issue be referred to the new Assembly.

The new General Assembly, meeting in Paris on 13 November, 1951, voted

37-11 not to debate a Soviet-sponsored bid for Communist representation of China. U.S. Secretary of State, Dean Acheson, said it would be "unthinkable" that the U.N. should discuss admitting Chinese Communists while they were killing U.N. troops in Korea. He said that Red China's international conduct was "so low that it would take considerable improvement to raise it to the general level of barbarism."[25] On 7 December, 1951, the Assembly rejected 39-7 a Russian resolution to declare the credentials of Chinese Nationalist U.N. delegates invalid.

In 1952, Russian efforts to oust Nationalist China from the United Nations failed on 17 October, when the Credentials Committee voted 6-3 (Russia, Sweden, and Burma opposed) to seat Nationalist delegates to the General Assembly. The Committee also approved a motion by U.S. Delegate Gross barring for the rest of the 1952 session "consideration of all proposals to exclude" the Nationalists, or to seat Red China's representative. There was no further significant discussion of the question during the Truman Administration.

It should be noted that Secretary Acheson originated the Uniting for Peace resolution. The United States had presented it to the United Nations on 3 November, 1950. This resolution shifted the center of gravity from the Security Council to the General Assembly, where the United States pretty much controlled the voting at the time. The United States was concerned with Russia's veto power. Under the Uniting for Peace resolution, if the Security Council failed to discharge its responsibilities because of a lack of unanimity among the permanent members, the General Assembly might consider the matter immediately. A majority in the General Assembly could vote for an emergency session to be held within twenty-four hours.

In 1952, President-elect Eisenhower nominated Henry Cabot Lodge as Ambassador to the United Nations. Eisenhower had pledged to go to Korea, if elected, and find a just and honorable peace.

In every U.N. Session from 1951 to 1961, the matter of Red China's admission was referred to a Steering Committee. General Assembly debate was deferred each year to the next year until 1961. In the United States there was an extremely hard line against admission of Red China to the United Nations. There was fear that a deal might be made to settle the Korean War. During the spring of 1953, Senator Jenner asked President Eisenhower to make a final statement that the United States would not sanction Red China's admission into the U.N. under any circumstances.

Secretary of State Dulles stated in 1953 that the Chinese Communists had not shown any desire to end their aggression in Korea. Therefore, they could not be considered for membership. At the Panmunjon Armistice Conference, China had wanted round-table discussions. They did not want the direct confrontation that a rectangular table enforced. China wanted Russia, India, Pakistan, Burma, and Indonesia to sit in as neutrals. The United States would not permit this.

A Korean Truce was finally signed on 27 July, 1953. Both sides claimed victory. United States' dead numbered 22,359—twice the number killed in World War I, but only about half of the men we have lost in Vietnam.

John Foster Dulles had written early in 1950, in his book *War and Peace*, that Communist China, if it proved its ability to govern China without serious domestic resistance, should be admitted to the United Nations.[26] He changed his view after Peking entered the Korean War. On 29 December, 1950, Dulles spoke to the American Association for the United Nations. He rejected former President Hoover's plan to withdraw United States defenses to the Western Hemisphere. Mr. Dulles spoke against admitting Communist China to the United Nations. He also announced a doctrine of massive retaliation. "The capacity to counter-attack is the ultimate deterrent."[27]

Dulles put no faith in the argument that admission to the United Nations would improve China's conduct. After the conclusion of the Japanese Peace Treaty early in 1951, Mr. Dulles resigned as U.S. Ambassador-at-Large. In a statement made on 24 May, 1951, Dulles stated that simple containment of Russian Communism was not enough. Asia was becoming what Stalin planned: the road to victory over the West.[28]

After the Korean settlement, the United States continued to oppose seating Communist China. A United Nations seat for Communist China would only give it more influence amongst its neighbors and adversely effect Cambodia through Vietnam to the Philippines. Chinese Communism would have to be contained until it gave up its objective of driving the United States from the western Pacific. It would not do any good to talk to China in the United Nations. We were talking to the Chinese Communists in Warsaw, and that did not do any good.[29]

A corollary to the doctrine of containment was aid to the Nationalist Government on Formosa. Members of the Congress felt that it was strategically correct to have Chiang ready to invade China to take advantage of a successful revolution on the mainland. United States strategy clutched at a straw conclusion, i.e. Chinese Communism's obvious evils were likely to be sufficient to destroy it.

At the Geneva Big Four Conference, early in 1955, there was some thawing in the Cold War. One month earlier, ex-president Truman had spoken in San Francisco at the 10th anniversary of the United Nations, urging disarmament. A general relaxation of international tension followed. Red China freed eleven American fliers captured in the Korean War. At the Foreign Ministers Conference, held that fall, agreement was reached on eighteen applicants to the U N. Mongolia, however, was vetoed by Nationalist China. Russia reciprocated and blocked the other seventeen applicants. Finally, sixteen nations went into the U.N. Mongolia and Japan were kept out. President Eisenhower appealed in vain to Chiang not to use the veto.

During most of the decade, 1951 to 1961, the United States kept Red China out of the U.N. without much difficulty.

Threats to leave the United Nations, or withhold financial support have been used more often than veto threats. President Eisenhower had to carry the brunt of these Congressional threats. Senator Everett M. Dirksen (R. Ill.) proposed a humiliating rider to a State Department Appropriation Bill, in May of 1953. The rider would have cut off the United States' one-third contribution to the United Nations' forty-million-dollar-a-year budget, if Red China were admitted to the United Nations. The Chairman, Styles Bridges, (R. N.H.) told the President that only three of the twenty-three committee members had voted against that rider. On the day the Bill was reported out of Committee, President Eisenhower told reporters he opposed both Red China's admission and the rider. Eisenhower had a showdown with the senators, and told them that the United States could not properly serve notice on the United Nations in such a manner, and more fundamentally, that the United States could not live alone.[30].

After a talk with the President, Senator William R. Knowland (R. Cal.) began to work toward a compromise. The senators decided to seek another way to show Congressional disapproval toward admitting Red China to the United Nations.[31] On 3 June, 1953, the Senate passed a resolution, 76-0, stating that it unqualifiedly opposed Red Chinese membership in the United Nations.

The following August, Senator Majority Leader Knowland, told California Republican leaders, in San Francisco, that he was giving "notice now" on the China question. He would move immediate action on a senate resolution that the United States leave the U.N. the day Communist China was admitted. On 18 August, 1953, Senator Alexander Wiley (R. Wis.), the Chairman of the Senate Foreign Relations Committee and a delegate to the General Assembly, issued a warning to other U.N. countries: a move to admit Red China would be a very serious matter to the American public and the Congress of the United States.[32]

On 8 July, 1954, Mr. Dulles was confident that the United States could keep Communist China from winning U.N. membership. When questioned about demands that the United States quit if Red China were seated, Dulles replied that he foresaw no American withdrawal from the United Nations or any occasion for it.[33] Dulles stated, however, that the United States would use the veto to bar Communist China in the U.N. Security Council and would demand a two-thirds vote in the U.N. General Assembly.

On this same day, under Administration pressure, Senator Knowland softened his attitude. He proposed legislation that if Red China became a member, the President should tell Congress the implications of this and any plans he had. On 13 July, 1954, the House Foreign Affairs Committee unanimously approved a resolution opposing Communist China's entry in the United Nations. But it was left to the Eisenhower Administration to decide what to do if Red China became a member.[34]

A few cracks in the American attitude developed in 1954. Senator Flanders (R. Vt.) commented that the United States should be willing to reconsider its objections when Communist China tore away its curtain and resumed free intercourse with the Western world. Dr. Charles Mayo, of the American U.N. Association, warned that the United States should review its policy from time to time. However, there was still a hard line in the Senate.

In a Washington interview, on 17 December, 1955, Senator Knowland demanded that Presidential aspirants in both parties state whether they would fight Communist China's admission to the United Nations, using the veto "if necessary." Knowland criticized the Eisenhower Administration for "acquiescence" in the 1955 package deal under which twelve non-Communist and four Communist nations entered the United Nations.[35] The veto of China, however, was not an issue in the 1956 presidential campaign.

In 1956, President Eisenhower proposed Massachusetts lawyer, Robert R. Bowie, as Assistant Secretary of State for Policy Planning. Senator Styles Bridges (R. N.H.), the Chairman of the G.O.P. Policy Committee, opposed Bowie because he had advocated a U.N. seat for Red China. Bowie denied the charge. He was then approved by the Senate Foreign Relations Committee.

The House of Representatives, on 17 August, 1957, voted 368-2 against admitting China, reiterating its opposition. A few years before, there had been no negative votes. Now there were two—Representatives Myer (D. Vt.) and Ashley (D. Oh.).

After the death of John Foster Dulles, Secretary Herter continued to oppose admitting Red China. Peking, according to Herter, was supporting efforts to subvert the will of free peoples. During the Chinese-Indian border clashes, Secretary Herter did concede that the China-Tibetan border was ill-defined and refused to take any sides. While reaffirming United States sympathy for India, he said that the United States lacked first-hand knowledge, particularly about the northwestern area with respect to the definitive border which could rightly be claimed by either side. The United States presumed that the claims of India were valid, but had only the word of a friend (India) to corroborate them.[36]

It seems as if President Eisenhower had strong support for his stand on China from his old World War II comrade and Chief, Sir Winston Churchill. President Eisenhower met Prime Minister Churchill in Bermuda at the onset of his administration. On several occasions Eisenhower and Churchill talked privately. Churchill had originally opposed British recognition of Red China. By 1953, his opposition had become habit and he had no intention of breaking it. He assured the President that he would always go along with the United States to bar Red China's admission to the United Nations. "After all," he said dryly, "we do prefer the United States over Red China as an ally."[37]

In September, 1960, President Eisenhower visited the United Nations. After addressing the General Assembly on 12 September, the President met with President Josip Broz Tito, of Yugoslavia. Tito seemed anxious to convince Eisenhower that he was not on the best terms with all members of the Communist bloc. "The Red Chinese," he said, "hate the Yugoslavs more vehemently than they hate the Americans." Despite this, Yugoslavia had supported admission of the Chinese Communists to the United Nations. It seemed only logical to admit a government that controlled a nation of six hundred million people.

"Our people feel a special animosity toward the Red Chinese Government," President Eisenhower answered, "for such good reasons as their invasion of South Korea and their holding and torturing some of our soldiers. Furthermore, they won't cease their persistent threats against Formosa, and their continual pressure on Southeast Asia. When I met with Khrushchev last year at Camp David, I told him that on that issue, the issue of Red China, we simply had to disagree."[38] President Tito seemed to understand this. He made quite a point of the affection that Yugoslavs felt for the United States.

President Kennedy brought a new approach to Chinese membership. Debate on the question would no longer be proscribed. The attitude of President Kennedy differed from the 1949 attitude of Congressman Kennedy. The young President was more somber than the Congressman of 1949. In the House, on 25 January, 1949, John F. Kennedy stated that the continued United States insistence that aid was not coming, unless a coalition were formed with the Communists, dealt a crippling blow to the National Government. Our diplomats and their advisers, the Lattimores and the Fairbanks, were too concerned with the imperfections of the democratic system in China. So concerned were they over tales of corruption in high places that they lost sight of our tremendous stake in non-Communist China. The tragic story of China was that we had tried to force Chiang and the Communists into a coalition. President Truman had treated Madame Chiang with indifference, if not contempt.[39]

President Kennedy was more responsible than Congressman Kennedy. At the start of the 16th Session, in 1961, the United States no longer opposed General Assembly debate on Chinese representation. The United States won Assembly endorsement on 15 December, 1961, by a 61-34 vote (7 abstentions), to make any substantive resolution dealing with Chinese representation an important question subject to a two-thirds majority vote.

The important-question maneuver was a parliamentary device to delay Communist China's membership originated by President Kennedy. He wanted debate, but did not want Red China to become a member until there had been a public-opinion shift in the United States. Mr. Sorenson has held that the China question was to be put off to the second term.

Under Article 18 of the Charter, decisions of the General Assembly on important questions shall be made by a 2/3 majority of the members present and voting. These important questions include the admission of new members. Under Article 4, the General Assembly cannot decide on members except those recommended by the Security Council. Under Article 27 of the Charter, as amended, Security Council decisions on all matters, except procedural ones, shall be made by an affirmative vote of eleven members, including the concurring votes of the permanent members.

At the 1961 General Assembly, the United States changed tactics. It cosponsored with Australia, Colombia, Italy, and Japan a resolution designating the Chinese representation issue an "important question." This resolution was adopted by a substantial majority of 61 in favor, 34 against, and 7 abstentions. The step was significant, because representation questions were normally considered a matter of credentials and were decided by a simple majority. Since "important questions" require a two-thirds' majority, this step forced proponents of Communist-Chinese representation to secure the support of two-thirds of the membership of the United Nations. Ambassador Stevenson had long argued, as a private citizen, that we must deal with realities, and perhaps move toward a solution which would seat both Chinese governments. Chester Bowles wanted to reconsider the whole China problem. Mr. Bowles strongly urged admitting the People's Republic of Mongolia to the United Nations.

In 1961, President Kennedy wanted to formulate parliamentary stratagems which might stall Peking's admission. Kennedy wanted to buy a year's time after 1961. Perhaps in 1962, the United States might begin preparing the way for Peking's admission. After 1962, the problem turned out not to be so pressing. In 1962, as in 1950, when an American President was preparing to reconsider the problem of Communist China, Peking itself elected a militant course. In 1950, China entered the Korean War. In 1962, China declared war on most of the world.[40]

President Kennedy considered the state of relations with Peking irrational. He never supposed that admission to the U.N. would work a miraculous conversion on the Chinese Communists. But there might be international gains if China entered the U.N. They would, however, be far outweighed by the uproar this would cause in domestic politics. Former President Eisenhower had told President Kennedy in their last meeting before the Inauguration that he hoped to support the new administration on all foreign-policy issues. Eisenhower, however, would consider it necessary to return to public life if Communist China threatened to enter the U.N. With his slim majorities in Congress and with the electorate, President Kennedy felt that he could not immediately take on the China problem.[41]

On 30 October 1962, a Soviet draft resolution calling for the ouster of the Nationalists was defeated by a vote of 56-42 (12 abstentions). This was the last time Russia sponsored Chinese membership. The next year, Albania sponsored Red China. The margin of defeat was slightly larger, 57-41 (12 abstentions). Under the two-thirds rule, 74 affirmative votes were required to seat Red China. During this debate, Mr. Fedorenko, of the Soviet Union, spoke in favor of Peking. He did not praise China, nor did he refer to the sponsoring speech by Albania's representative, Mr. Shytlla.

By 1963, President Kennedy and Prime Minister MacMillan concluded that China presented the long-term danger to peace. China was increasingly on the minds of every one, except those in the Department of State, who were "still babbling about the Sino-Soviet bloc."[42]

During the summer of 1963, President Kennedy and Premier Khrushchev concluded a nuclear test ban treaty in Moscow. Kennedy and Khrushchev both lost battles to sign up de Gaulle and Chairman Mao.

After the United Nations General Assembly rejected the 1963 attempt to seat Red China, Ambassador Stevenson said that the vote revealed the Assembly's strong aversion to Peking. A few days later, on 24 October, United Nations Day, Ambassador Stevenson went to Dallas for a meeting. The National Indignation Convention countered his visit with a "United States Day." General Edwin A. Walker was the principal speaker and denounced the United Nations. That evening, Walker patriots went to the auditorium to heckle Stevenson. While being heckled, Stevenson remarked with customary poise "for my part, I believe in the forgiveness of sin, and the redemption of ignorance."[43]

The one major foreign-policy issue deliberately postponed to the second term of the Kennedy Administration was Red China.[44]

France recognized the People's Republic of China in January, 1964. The United States made a strong protest. There was no 1964 vote on the question in the United Nations due to the "no voting" policy. The United States was ready to attempt to deny the vote to the Soviet Union under Article 19 of the Charter. This was the so-called assessment crisis. The United States held that the Charter would be flagrantly violated if Article 19 were not applied against the Soviet Union simply because it was a great power. All assembly action was approved by acclamation. The confrontation between the United States and the U.S.S.R., over vote deprivation, was postponed until January, 1965.

On 8 December, 1964, Irish External Affairs Minister, Frank Aiken, said that peace would be strengthened if Communist China had a permanent Security Council seat. He opposed, however, ousting Nationalist China from the U.N. At this time, Indian Foreign Minister Sardar Swaran Singh assailed Communist China for its attacks on India's border. India still favored admission of the People's Republic of China to the U.N., even though 14 to 15 Chinese divisions were poised on the Indian frontier.

On 16 August, 1965, Ambassador Goldberg announced that the United States would no longer demand that voting rights in the U.N. General Assembly be denied to members who were more than two years in arrears in paying their assessments for United Nations peace-keeping expenses. The United States recognized that a majority of the members were simply unwilling to apply Article 19 and did not wish to frustrate the consensus. Regular voting was resumed at the 20th Session of the General Assembly. The United States agreed to voluntary payments. Also, the United States reserved the same option to take exception to the principle of collective financial responsibility with respect to certain activities of the Organization. That is, the United States would not commit itself to paying for peace-keeping operations which it did not approve.

Pope Paul VI addressed the General Assembly on 4 October, 1965, urging U.N. members to unite in their pact those nations who did not yet share in it.[45] Ambassador Goldberg reiterated United States opposition to admitting Communist China. Britain and France took strong steps in favor of such admission during the General Assembly debate on 7 October, 1965. On 17 November, 1965, the 117-member U.N. General Assembly defeated by a 47-47 vote (20 abstentions) a resolution to seat Communist China and expel Nationalist China. Under the important-question rule, a two-thirds' majority of members present and voting was needed to expel a member.

Supporters of Communist China's admission considered the tie vote a considerable victory for their side. Many observers speculated that if the resolution for admission of Communist China had not been worded in such a way that the Nationalists would lose their seat, it would have received a clear majority. An amendment to this effect was proposed shortly before the voting by the Ceylon and Mauritania delegations. Cambodia and Albania, sponsors of the original resolution, asked them to withdraw it. The amended resolution, instead of calling for the expulsion of Nationalist China along with Peking's admission, would have stated only that "the representatives of the People's Republic of China be seated in the United Nations and all its organs." According to the sponsors of the original resolution, the Peking government insisted on the expulsion of Nationalist China as a precondition for accepting admission in the United Nations; therefore, the original resolution was not changed.[46]

The United Nations would not admit Red China as a member, but on 20 November, 1965, by 112-0 vote, with France abstaining, and Nationalist China not participating, the U.N. General Assembly adopted a resolution calling for a world disarmament conference that would include Communist China. Ten days later, on 1 December, the Foreign Ministry in Peking released a statement that China would certainly not take part in the U.N.-proposed disarmament conference. It asserted that China would never enter into any U.N. conferences until her legitimate rights had been restored in the United Nations, and the Chiang Kai-shek clique expelled.

On 12 July, 1966, President Johnson assured Communist China that the United States sought a peace of conciliation, not of conquest, in Asia. All United States' overtures to China would be continued, even though China had so far spurned them all. The President's address was described by White House officials as his first major statement on Communist China.[47] The next month, President Johnson told the American Legion Convention, in Washington, that the United States could not safely assume that Communist China's militant words were only rhetoric. The President anticipated the day when those on mainland China, who were ready to meet us halfway, would peacefully take their place as one of the major world powers. It was reported on 8 September, 1966, that Communist Chinese Foreign Minister, Chen Yi, had told visiting Japanese Diet Members that China did not desire a clash with the United States. In the West, there were optimistic reactions to Chen's statements. Later, Peking said China had no intention of talking to the United States about peace in Vietnam.[48]

Secretary of State Rusk responded, at a Washington news conference on 16 September, 1966, that the United States would continue to oppose Communist China's membership in the United Nations. The United States would continue its efforts towards an eventual reconciliation with Communist China through concentration on visitors' exchanges.[49] There was a little thaw, but the ice formed again quickly.

On 16 November 1966, ten sponsors presented a resolution calling for Communist China's entry into the United Nations. The resolution called on the Assembly to "restore all rights" to Red China. As worded, the resolution raised only the question of which of the two Chinese Governments should represent all of China in the U.N. It did not invoke admitting or expelling a state. Once again, it was voted an important question requiring a two-thirds' majority.

On 29 November, 1966, the 121-member General Assembly defeated a resolution to seat Communist China by a vote of 57-46 (17 abstained). An Italian proposal to appoint a special committee to investigate Red China's position with regard to U.N. membership was defeated on the same day, 62-34 (25 abstentions). The Canadian proposal to seat Communist China as a permanent member of the Security Council, with Nationalist China as a member of the General Assembly, was never intended by Canadian External Affairs Minister, Martin, to be put to a vote. It was intended to stimulate new thinking.

At the opening of the General Assembly, in September, Ambassador Goldberg said categorically that it was not the policy of the United States to isolate Communist China from the world. The international community could not countenance Peking's doctrine and policy of intervening by violence and subversion in other nations. Two facts were important to the United States' attitude. The Republic of China on Taiwan was a founding member of the United Nations. Any effort to exclude it from the United Nations in order to seat representatives of Communist China in their place would be vigorously opposed by the United States. The second fact was that Communist China, unlike any one else in the organization, had put forward extraordinary terms for consenting to enter the United Nations. Communist China demanded that the Charter be changed to its satisfaction. To this, the United States could not consent.[50]

In his State-of-the-Union Message, on 10 January, 1967, President Johnson said that we would be the first to welcome a China which decided to respect her neighbor's rights. We, in the United States, would be the first to applaud if China would apply her great energies to improving the welfare of her own people. America had no intention of trying to deny China's legitimate needs for security and friendly relations with her neighboring countries. Our hope that this would some day come about rested on the conviction that the American people would see Vietnam through to an honorable peace.[51]

The seventeenth annual China debate at the United Nations, in 1967, was essentially a formality. The United States, with a substantial assist from Peking, scored again in its annual crusade to bar Peking. The defeat of the China Resolution represented the triumph of the absurd. Communist behavior in the period just before the 1967 vote discouraged Peking's supporters. The chaos of the cultural revolution assured the United States a substantial majority in blocking admission In addition, the Sino-Soviet dispute deprived Peking of anything more than *pro forma* support from Russia and its Communist allies. Once again, in 1968, the same formula was followed. Perhaps the representatives from Turtle Bay did not find China as chaotic in 1968 as in 1967. However, the vote was essentially the same.[52]

Peking indicated to the world in 1968 that China, the ancient center of the universe, could stand alone in the modern world. On the United States' side, a few major cracks developed. Responsible citizens had been saying that important question was not answered by votes. The big question was how to bring China back into the community of nations. That question remains for the Nixon Administration.

United Nations delegations showed a deep interest in the recent United States election. It appears that few delegates actually mourned the departure of President Johnson. The Vietnam War and Mr. Johnson were identical. The conflict is still quite unpopular with United Nations delegates. This attitude may help President Nixon. Generally speaking, Mr. Nixon was not a favorite of the United Nations delegations, particularly the European ones. However, the invasion of Czechoslovakia changed all that. The chancelleries of Europe were alarmed. Thus, the presence of a hardliner in the White House is no longer as repugnant as it once was.

In regard to the Soviets, President Nixon made a quick turnaround from hard-line oratory. During the campaign, Mr. Nixon spoke repeatedly of "superiority." We are now hearing of "sufficiency." These are hard words to follow, but, at least, they indicate a willingness to come and reason together. No such real willingness to reason has been demonstrated toward China. We have started talks once again with China in Warsaw. But how much value will they have? In President Nixon's first press conference, he took a negative tone toward relations with Communist China. In answer to a question, the President emphasized that this country's long opposition to Peking's admission to the United Nations remained unchanged. That was pretty emphatic in Washington, and seems to have been heard emphatically in Peking, also.

In the fall of 1968, prospects seemed better. Communist China seemed to be moving into a quieter phase of the cultural revolution. Propaganda organs still insist that the ranks must continually be cleaned up. This euphemism evidently covers factional infighting. In the past few years, the fanatic violence of the unrestrained Red Guards predominated. That seems to have passed to a new stage of individual infighting for power.

In November, 1968, a 1949 report on conditions in China was re-issued. The 1949 report emphasized moderation in political policy, and production and development in the economic sphere.[53]

On 15 February, 1969, Senator Hugh Scott, speaking in Tokyo, stated that the Nixon Administration had new options in developing policy toward Communist China. The Pennsylvania Republican suggested that American opinion could be guided in the direction of broadening negotiations with mainland China. On the basis of Japanese advice, the Senator stated that, in his opinion, China was a closed society, and that we could not get at the pearl until we had found a means of opening the oyster. Many Japanese Diet Members commented in private that they were pleased and surprised to find their American Congressional visitors taking a flexible, nondogmatic approach, not only to Okinawa, but to China as well. Mr. Scott suggested that the Nixon Administration renew the Johnson Administration's proposal for journalistic and cultural exchanges with Communist China. In addition, new proposals could be tried out in the Warsaw ambassadorial talks between the United States and Communist China.[54]

The annual U.N. fiasco debate and vote on China in November, 1969 took place with a new background. Canada, Italy, and perhaps Belgium were willing to establish full diplomatic relations with China if an agreement could be worked out. Peking has demanded Canada recognize that Communist China includes Formosa. Canada does not seem to mind breaking relations with Formosa, but it does not consider itself obliged to accept all of Peking's territorial claims.

At the United Nations in November, 1969, many diplomats felt that the worst was over in China. The Chinese Communist government would now tend toward a more reasonable and flexible attitude. The diplomats felt that the cultural Revolution had blown itself out. The main problem at the U.N. remains, however, how to admit one Chinese government without expelling the other.

Regardless of softening attitudes, the U.N. General Assembly rejected Peking for the 20th year. In the key 1969 vote, 48 nations supported the pro-Peking resolution and 56 opposed it. Belgium, Canada and Italy, and 18 other nations, abstained.

President Nixon made his maiden speech to the United Nations in September of 1969. Mr. Nixon deplored China's self-imposed isolation, and he assured the delegates that the United States is ready to talk to Peking. The official line of Mr. Nixon and Mr. Rogers is that China's isolation from the world community is of its own making. This is a softer line than previous United States policy. It would seem that the United States may abstain on the question in future years, if there is any progress in the Warsaw talks, and if the domestic political situation allows Mr. Nixon to bow out in such a graceful manner from the adamant position we have maintained since the Korean War.

Will Mr. Nixon be able to bow out so gracefully? It does not seem so now in the spring of 1970 with the recent domestic bitterness over the Carswell nomination to the Supreme Court.

Why did Mr. Nixon make such an obvious blunder? Can such a man pull the United States out of Vietnam, and bring Peking into the concert of nations? Perhaps. Mr. Nixon seems to find strength in failure. He can fail in such a case as the Carswell nomination, and triumph in his own resolution to triumph over adversity.

A marvelous opportunity to settle a number of international problems may be approaching. Perhaps the open way in which our space program has been handled has built up good will which had been draining rapidly in Vietnam. The emblem of Apollo 13 was a troika of horses and the unprophetic motto: "Ex Luna, Scientia." Actually, the mechanical failure which prevented the moonlanding, and endangered the lives of the astronauts, may have brought more good than a successful mission. People all over the world agonized over the fate of Apollo 13. The return of Captain Lovell and crew demonstrated primarily character, competence, and courage by cool, calm, capable men. The day these men returned to earth also brought a hint of peace from Jacob A. Malik, the Soviet delegate to the United Nations.

Phillip Jessup met Mr. Malik by accident at the U.N. in February, 1949. Dr. Jessup used the unexpected opportunity to ask a deliberate question on the Berlin Blockade. Mr. Malik was willing to ask Moscow for fresh instructions, and in due time, the blockade was lifted.

George Kennan called on Mr. Malik in May, 1951, after the Korean War had been raging for about a year. General MacArthur had been removed just before this meeting. Evidently, Mr. Kennan and Mr. Malik were able to reach an understanding. Within a month Mr. Malik made a vaguely worded call for a cease-fire and armistice talks in Korea. President Truman immediately replied that the United States was willing to engage in such talks. On 29 June, 1951, General Ridgway broadcast an offer to negotiate an armistice.

Now, almost twenty years later, Mr. Malik has dropped another hint. He told reporters at the U.N. at the time of the Apollo 13 space-flight that the real situation in Vietnam et. al. now calls for a new Geneva Conference to bring about a new solution and to relax tensions in the peninsula of Indo-China.

For years overtures have been made to the Soviets on this issue without success. The British and the Americans have suggested new Indo-Chinese conferences. Until now, the Soviet Union either ignored or rejected all overtures without hesitation. The war clouds may be beginning to break up.

The Soviet Union has a deep and a growing fear of China. The border incidents of 1969 have shown that war is possible. The Soviets apparently threatened Peking with a nuclear strike and forced them to the conference table. But the conference has made no progress. Now there is a new situation in Indo-China. Ho Chi Minh is dead, and those who are winning the power struggle in Hanoi may be moving toward China. Prince Sihanouk has been ousted in Cambodia and is using Peking as his base, as he plans counterrevolution.

Meanwhile, the United States and the Soviet Union made enough progress at Helsinki to open a second round of SALT talks at Vienna. A Geneva conference on Indo-China could help the Russians retrieve some influence in Vietnam and save them money in the arms race. A diplomatic settlement, producing genuinely independent nations in Indo-China, would prevent Peking from dominating the whole peninsula.

Such a settlement might set the stage for progress in SALT II, the Strategic Arms Limitation Talks, that resumed in Vienna in April, 1970. With progress in Vietnam, and in the arms race, it would only be another step to bring Peking to the United Nations, and then start work on an international universal agreement to control nuclear energy.

FOOTNOTES

[1] Truman, Harry S., Memoirs, Vol. II, Years of Trial and Hope, 1946-1952 (New York: Doubleday & Company, Inc., 1956) p. 337.
[2] The Honorable Paul Martin, Speech at the Twenty-first Session of the United Nations General Assembly, 23 November, 1966, Canada, Department of External Affairs Press Release, p. 4.
[3] Hull, Cordell, The Memoirs of Cordell Hull, Vol. II (New York: The MacMillan Company, 1948) p. 1666.
[4] Facts on File, Vol. X, 1950, p. 346.
[5] Facts on File, Vol. XV, 1955, p. 424.

[6]Truman, Harry S., *op. cit.*, p. 364.

[7]*Ibid.*, p. 354.

[8]*Ibid.*, p. 355.

[9]*Ibid.*, p. 362.

[10]*Ibid.*, p. 372.

[11]*Ibid.*, p. 373.

[12]*Ibid.*, p. 383.

[13]*Ibid.*, p. 402.

[14]*Ibid.*, p. 408.

[15]*Ibid.*, p. 416.

[16]*Ibid.*, p. 442.

[17]Bundy, McGeorge, ed., *The Pattern of Responsibility* (Boston: Houghton Mifflin Company, 1952) p. 270.

[18]Truman, Harry S., *op. cit.*, p. 429.

[19]Facts on File, Vol. X, 1950, p. 424.

[20]*Ibid.*, p. 424.

[21]*Ibid.*, p. 398.

[22]Facts on File, Vol. XI, 1951, p. 178.

[23]*Ibid.*, p. 417.

[24]*Ibid.*, p. 155.

[25]*Ibid.*, p. 363.

[26]Eisenhower, Dwight D., *Mandate for Change 1953-1956* (New York: Doubleday and Company, Inc., 1963) p. 249.

[27]Facts on File, Vol. X, 1950, p. 425.

[28]Facts on File, Vol. XXII, 1952, p. 169.

[29]Burding, Andrew H., *Dulles on Diplomacy* (New York: D. Van Nostrand Company, 1965) p. 57.

[30]Eisenhower, *Memoirs*, Vol. I, p. 214.

[31]*Ibid.*, p. 215.

[32]Facts on File, Vol. XXIII, 1953, p. 269.

[33]Facts on File, Vol., XIV, 1954, p. 234.

[34]*Ibid.*, p. 235.

[35]Facts on File, Vol. XX, 1960, p. 369.

[36]Facts on File, 1959, Vol. XIX, p. 371.

[37]Eisenhower, Dwight D., *Mandate for Change*, p. 249.

[38]Eisenhower, Dwight D., *Waging Peace 1959-1961* (New York: Doubleday and Company, Inc., 1965) p. 584.

[39]Kennedy, John F., *Statements and Speeches Made During Service in Senate and House*, Senate Document 79, 88th Congress, 2nd Session (Washington: U. S. Government Printing Office, 1964) p. 41.

[40]Schlesinger, Arthur M., *A Thousand Days* (Boston: Houghton Mifflin Company, 1965) p. 480.

[41]*Ibid.*, p. 479.

[42]*Ibid.*, p. 903.

[43]*Ibid.*, p. 1020.

[44]Sorensen, Theodore C., *Kennedy* (New York: Harper & Row, 1965) p. 755.

[45]Facts on File, 1965, Vol. XXV, p. 354.

[46]Leng, Russell J., *Chinese Representation in the United Nations* (Washington: The Library of Congress, Legislative Reference Service, Foreign Affairs Division, 6 December, 1965) p. 9.

[47]Facts on File, 1966, Vol. XXVI, p. 252.

[48]*Ibid.*, p. 340.

[49]*Ibid.*, p. 363.

[50]Goldberg, Arthur J., Address to the General Assembly, United Nations, 22 September, 1966.

[51]Facts on File, 1967, Vol. XXVII, p. 5.

[52]*New York Times*, 6 October, 1968, p. 13.

[53]*New York Times*, 26 November, 1968, p. 13.

[54]*New York Times*, 15 February, 1969, p. 13.

CHAPTER VI

AMERICAN AND WORLDWIDE PUBLIC OPINION

American Public Opinion

Presidents Kennedy, Eisenhower, and Truman all expressed their respect for the power of public opinion about Chinese membership in the United Nations. Each president felt that his hands were tied by public opinion. How do the people feel on the issue? How did the people feel towards President Truman and General MacArthur? The problem originated with the Korean War. General MacArthur was ready to risk World War III in his Korean campaigns. The Commander-in-Chief of the United States was not ready to take that risk. Those people who preferred General MacArthur to President Truman are generally those who have followed a strong, hard line against admission of the People's Republic to the United Nations. Those who preferred President Truman are inclined to have been more conciliatory.

The Gallup Opinion Index asks a "most-admired man" question each year in December. The question is as follows:

"What man that you have heard or read about living in any part of the world, do you admire the most?"[1]

Each year the top ten are listed. Truman and MacArthur were ranked as follows:[2]

	President Truman	General MacArthur
1946	3	1
1947	4	1
1948	1	3
1949	1	4
1950	3	2
1951	3	1
1952	4	2
1953	4	3
1954	5	6
1955	4	3
1956	-	6
1957	3	7
1958	5	6
1959	4	10

1960	8	10
1961	6	10
1962	7	6
1963	-	-
1964	-	-
1965	10	-
1966	-	-

These figures speak for themselves. It is obvious that General MacArthur did fade away faster than President Truman. After the General's death, in 1964, President Truman's name came back onto the list. The President had more staying power with the American people. General MacArthur was one of the ten most admired men for seventeen years, one year longer than the former President. Mr Truman's name came back after an absence of two years. This is a strong indication of his enduring influence on American public opinion.

Shortly before the Korean Armistice, in 1953, a substantial majority of the American public disapproved giving Red China a seat on the United Nations Security Council. A majority of the British public approved it, according to the British Institute of Public Opinion. Fifty-two per cent of those questioned in Britain thought that China should be admitted as a member of the United Nations.[3]

In the United States, two years later, the admission of Communist China to the United Nations, so overwhelmingly opposed by the general public, had the backing of the nation's top citizens in two professions—education and religion. A special poll of names, included in Who's Who in America, indicated that the group as a whole was almost 2-1 against admitting the Chinese Communists. Leaders in business and industry were overwhelmingly opposed. An Indiana educator replied that Communist China represented the government of the Chinese people, whether we like it or not.[4]

In 1954, with the situation in Southeast Asia becoming increasingly grave, 62% of those polled thought it would be a good idea to build up a U.N. emergency force of a size sufficient to fight "brushfire" wars. The United States had recently suggested that a United Nations emergency force be sent to Southeast Asia to settle border disputes in that area. A strong U.N. Army large enough to be used in settling international disputes has long had solid support from the United States public.[5]

In the fall of 1955, 71% of the American people thought that Communist China should not be a member of the United Nations. 17% were for representation and 12% had no opinion. The public was also of the opinion that, even if a majority of the other members decided to admit Peking, the United States should not go along with the decision.[6] This would imply support for a veto by the

United States, but, of course, the people polled did not all think that out. On both questions, there was virtually no difference of opinion between Republicans and Democrats. Independent voters were inclined to be slightly more sympathetic to Red China's admission. However, only 33% of the Independents supported admission.

In June, 1955, 57% of the people polled did not think the United States should resign if a majority of the other U.N. members voted to admit Red China. A large percentage of the people—26%—had no opinion.[7]

In 1961, as debate began again in the General Assembly, a nationwide Gallup poll found virtually no change in the public's basic position that the Red Chinese did not merit a seat. There was a substantial increase in those who would acquiesce in a vote for Chinese admission by a majority of United Nations members. In 1955, 31% would go along. By 1961, 46% held that the United States should go along with a U.N. decision.[8]

During the severe food famine of 1962 in China, 48% of the people polled thought that the United States should send food. 60% of those polled also thought that the United Nations should try to solve the problem of feeding and resettling famine refugees.[9]

By the spring of 1966, the public's "vote" in favor of seating Red China was 25% in favor (the word "vote" used by Gallup). In five years, those in favor of Chinese admission increased by about 40% from 18% in 1961 to 25% in 1966. Although the public has consistently opposed seating Red China in the United Nations, the public would favor admission by a 2-1 vote, if they could be convinced that this would improve relations between Red China and the United Stated.

College-trained persons were most in favor of admission—about two persons in three of this group. Republicans, within the college-trained group, expressed less support than did Democrats, but Independents of the group were most in favor of admission. Younger persons, 21 to 29, were predominantly on the side of admitting Red China, if it would help improve relations with that country.[10]

The strongest opposition came from those people living in communities with a population of 50,000 to 499,999. Of those polled in such communities only 19% felt that Communist China should become a U.N. member. Nationwide, the Republicans were stronger for a Communist Chinese U.N. seat than Democrats (Republicans 27% for; Democrats 23%). The percentage of Independents for was higher than both—28% More Catholics were for a seat than Protestants by 5% (27-22). Opposition was strongest in the Midwest, the South, and in the $3,000-$5,000-income group.[11]

It has been reported in the press on occasion that a person's opinion on Chinese admission is fast becoming a status symbol. To be in favor of Red China's admission to the United Nations is an "in" position.

World Opinion

Chinese foreign policy has been most ambitious in the face of severe interna shortcomings. Despite prolonged economic crisis, and a legacy of poverty, back wardness, and civil war, Red China has thrown down the gauntlet before major anc minor powers. More than ever before, Peking has become a disturbing challenge tc United States policymakers. Again and again, the Chinese-Communist Party was driven to the brink of extinction. Again and again, it returned to fight another day and eventually to win. The 19th century in China was one of humiliation. The 20th century has been one of chaos, misery, and, finally, of success and isolation The United States policy of exclusion has succeeded in the United Nations. Withir China, it has been a flag with which to rally the people. In the past seventeer years, through monumental feats of organization, China's Communist leaders have imposed unity and discipline on a country which had known little of either for 125 years. United States opposition has been a bond of Chinese unity. The United States policy has substantiated fictions in the minds of those on Taiwan, and has inflamed hatred in the minds of those on mainland-China.

For many years the United States has aborted its good will among nations by its inflexible opposition to Peking. For a period of ten years, the United States successfully fought debate on the subject in the United Nations. Free speech discussion, and debate are considered to be important attributes of the American way of life. Many of our allies consider the United States "no debate position" to be theoretically absurd, and hypocritical. America has preached about free speech yet it has opposed debate on the China question until recent years.

The United States has isolated China. In doing so, America has partially isolated itself from traditional allies. Many of America's partners in the North Atlantic Alliance vote for Red China's admission to the U.N.

In the fall of 1966, Canada shifted from a pro-United States position to abstention. The Netherlands, also, abstained. All the following trading partners and historical friends of the United States voted contrary to our position: Britain, Norway, Denmark, Sweden, and Finland. In isolating Red China, the United States has isolated itself and has also lost good will within the North Atlantic community. These nations are also opposed to United States involvement in Vietnam. The United States has so isolated itself that it is having no success in bringing the Vietnamese War to the United Nations in search of a solution.

Canada and Italy will probably establish diplomatic relations with Peking in the near future. Talks have begun in Sweden between Canadian and Chinese officials. The Trudeau government made overtures to Peking early in February, 1969. The Canadian Government has so far found a measure of optimism in Peking's official silence. In 1966, Canada proposed that both Communist China and Nationalist China should be United Nations members. Peking quickly rejected this proposal.[12]

The United States expressed concern that the Canadian moves toward recognizing Communist China could imperil the international position of the National Chinese Government on Taiwan. Washington and Ottawa have been in regular consultation on China policies ever since Prime Minister Trudeau suggested last May that Canada might open diplomatic relations with the mainland government. It does not appear that opposition from the United States will deter the Trudeau government.

Another member of the North Atlantic Treaty Organization has indicated intentions of recognizing Communist China. The Italian Government announced on 24 January, 1969, that it was investigating diplomatic procedures for exchanging embassies with Peking. The United States position has been expressed to Italy, also. The United States firmly supports the Nationalist Government, despite mounting sentiment in Congress and in the academic community.[13]

It appears that Italy and Canada are trying to force the hand of the United States. This is not at all surprising. Italy and Canada have initiated new moves in this area for many years. United States officials do not seem to be too worried over the recent overtures. The Nixon Administration has warned that any enhancement of Peking's stature would endanger the security of Eastern Asia. This warning seems somewhat laconic. It appears that State Department officials do not expect recognition to come quickly. Relations with Taiwan are always delicate and troublesome during talks with Peking. For years, both Chinese Governments have insisted that no foreign government can recognize both Chinese regimes.

The following statements constitute an indicative sample of world opinion on the question, as of October, 1966:

Cambodia

The two-China theory cannot be considered. There is only one China, just as there can be only one Canada, or Italy, or only one United States of America. In accordance with the Cairo Declaration of 1943, the Islands of Formosa and the Pescadores should be returned to China. That decision was reaffirmed in the Japanese Peace Treaty of 1951. In December of 1954, the United States of America signed a "treaty of mutual defense" with the Chiang Kai-shek clique. In January, 1955, the Senate adopted a resolution authorizing President Eisenhower to use the Armed Forces to protect Formosa from armed attack.

These two documents were signed after Chiang had fled the continent of China. This constitutes glaring proof that the U.S.A. has violated the principles of the U.N. Charter. America has arrogated to itself the right to interfere in the internal affairs of the Chinese people.[14]

Canada

The Canadian delegation feels that this question cannot be resolved as long as the parties proceed on the narrow concept of votes. A solution should be sought in terms of consensus. The issue cannot be shelved much longer. The study commit-tee proposal before them represents little forward motion from the 1950 Canadian proposal. China is a member state. The issue is not membership. Rather, the issue is how can China, as a member state, be represented in such a way as to reflect the realities of the present situation. With these practical requirements in mind the Canadian Delegation suggests the following guidelines as the basis for a reasonable solution:

1. The participation of the Republic of China in the U.N. General Assembly as a member representing the territory over which it exercises effective jurisdiction.

2. The participation of the People's Republic of China in the UNGA as mem-ber representing the territory over which it exercises effective jurisdiction.

3. The participation of the People's Republic of China in the Security Council as a permanent member.[15]

Chile

The Chilean delegation does not agree with either of the two positions. There is no desire to prevent the participation of the People's Republic of China in the United Nations. However, they cannot turn a blind eye to the fate of millions of people on Formosa. Representatives of the Peking Government have issued state-ments adverse to the United Nations. Chile does not accept those judgments. It believes they should be condemned. However, Chile does not believe that from those words it can deduce the future attitude of that country. Up to this moment, there has been no invitation to the People's Republic of China to participate in the United Nations. So long as the door is kept shut, a benevolent attitude cannot be expected from a country that has been excluded from this organization for so many years.

Nationalist China

In view of what has been taking place in China, and of the regime's attitude toward the rest of the world, it behooves all members of the Assembly—including those of the Soviet Bloc—to ask themselves whether it is in the interest of their respective countries, or in the interest of the United Nations, to allow this unre-generate regime to occupy China's seat in the United Nations. The Chinese Com-munist regime in Peking has made no secret of its contempt and detestation of the United Nations. Peking has called for the Charter to be revised and for the expul-sion of "imperialist puppets."

The Chinese Communist hostility towards the Soviet Union has reached the point of no return. If the Communist Chinese can regard their antagonism for the Soviet Union as irreconcilable, is there any ground for believing that the seating of the Peking Regime would diminish by an iota its hostility toward the United Nations? The Representative of Cambodia speaks glowingly of Peking's dedication to peace. I wonder whether he really means what he says. Is he blind to Peking's aggressive deeds and deaf to Peking's bellicose words? The Chinese Communists abjure "peaceful co-existence." They have never concealed their abomination for it. It is precisely on this issue that they have taken the Soviet Union to task. This is what they mean when they talk about "Khrushchev revisionism."

In recent months, Mao Tse-tung's Red Guards have been beating people to death with sticks. The populace has been subjected to horrible indignities and humiliation. Temples, art treasures, and cherished old monuments have been ripped down. Mao would not have resorted to such drastic measures if he had not felt that his regime was in grave danger of collapsing. The official press now openly admits that the "cultural revolution" has encountered "stubborn resistance." There is reason for believing that even the "People's Liberation Army," on which the regime depends to keep itself in power, is being plagued by internal conflict and dissension. All this underscores the undeniable fact that the regime is falling apart. It has no longer any effective control over either the masses of the people or the Party apparatus itself. The proponents of the two-China theory profess the friendliest feelings towards that Government which I have the honor to represent. Let me state with all the emphasis at my command that there are not "two Chinas." The Chinese people recognize only one China, and only one legal government of China.[16] The government of the Republic of China—it is to that Government that the suffering masses on the mainland look for their eventual deliverance. The Chinese people are facing tragic, fateful times. If the United Nations cannot help the Chinese people to regain their freedom, let it at least refrain from giving aid and comfort to its enslavers.[17]

Italy

For more than a decade, the question of Chinese admission has been debated. 700 million Chinese still are not represented in the United Nations. Peking administers and governs the whole of mainland-China. Conclusive discussion of the question is inhibited because we do not know the intentions of the Peking Government. Does the People's Republic of China really want to be represented in the United Nations? Assuming an affirmative reply, is that Government prepared to comply with the Charter of the United Nations?[18]

Malaysia

The problem of Chinese representation should be discussed with a view of exploring ways to a solution. The absence of the People's Republic of China has often been cited as a glaring example of the lack of universality. The government of Malaysia has always believed that the Chinese people, with their illustrious civilization, should be brought into the association. It is a fact, however, that the People's Republic of China, by choosing to adopt critical and even hostile policies toward the United Nations, has created barriers in its own path. Peking has demanded that the organization be re-shaped in a manner acceptable to it. We regret

China's attitude. No single nation can impose its will on the United Nations. This question can only be considered with the question of the fate of the 13 million inhabitants of Taiwan. They must not be denied the right to pursue a destiny of their own.[19]

Malawi

The Malawi Governments feels unable to subscribe to a policy which denies all recognition to the People's Republic of China. A government which is clearly in effective control of a country consisting of over four million square miles of land, with a population of over 700 million people, cannot be ignored and must be recognized as such. However, admission of the People's Republic of China must be conditional upon that government demonstrating convincingly to existing member states that it has a genuine intention to observe the rules and the spirit of the United Nations Charter. The utterances and actions of that government's leaders have yet to convince us. Further, the admission of Peking must not result in the eviction of the government of Taiwan.[20]

Mongolia People's Republic

Mongolia regrets American Imperialism in Vietnam and Korea. The delegation notes with regret that the principles of universality in the United Nations have been violated by certain member states in their selfish interests. The Mongolian delegation considers that the legitimate rights of the People's Republic of China should be restored immediately. The representatives of Chiang Kai-shek's clique must be expelled from all organs of the United Nations. The principle of universality should also be applied to the question of admitting observers. Here, again, the delegation witnesses discrimination. The United States has abused the advantage of being the host country to the United Nations' headquarters.[21]

Nepal

Since 1 October, 1949, China has been governed by the People's Republic of China. This government is the only legitimate government of China. Until 1949, it was a backward, exploited and weak country. In the past seventeen years, it has become a power with which to be reckoned. It is a rapidly developing strong nuclear power. Others say that China is arrogant and aggressive. Nepal has not found that this is the case. A happy relationship exists between the Kingdom of Nepal and the People's Republic of China. It is based on equality, noninterference, mutual respect, and peaceful coexistence. Like all of China's small neighboring states, Nepal was able to carry out negotiations on the border questions. They had remained unsolved for over a century. The boundary agreement which was eventually signed by His Majesty, King Mahendra, and His Excellency, President Liu Shao-chi, of China, brought back to Nepal 300 square miles of territory which was formerly in dispute. This boundary agreement is a shining example of Nepal's relations with the People's Republic of China.[22]

New Zealand

Mainland-China has lain under the control of the Peking Government since 1949. The Republic of China also remains in existence on the Island of Taiwan. Its population of some 12 million people, although small in comparison with that of mainland-China, remains substantially greater in size than the population of the majority of member states of this organization, including New Zealand. There are powerful arguments in favor of the Peking Government in this organization. What is the price of Peking's participation? This is the substance of the difficulty. Peking insists that the United Nations expel the Republic of China. This is not a price the Assembly has been disposed to pay, nor should it. On 26 September, 1965, Marshal Chen Yi said, at his press conference, that the United Nations "must rectify its mistakes and undergo a thorough organization and reform. . . and all the imperialist puppets should be expelled." This is hardly a prescription for accommodation or reconciliation.

New Zealand is conscious of the potential significance of Communist China. It would welcome an understanding between Peking and the non-Communist world. They look forward to some acceptable opening of the present impasse. Peking's participation is not a goal to be sought at any price. New Zealand cannot agree that Nationalist China can be abandoned. Nor can it agree that the United Nations should be "re-tooled," reformed, purged, or anything else as a condition of Peking's presence in it.[23]

Norway

To make the United Nations an effective instrument of international co-operation, Norway has held that the organization should admit as member states all sovereign countries which are willing and in a position to join it. Norway adheres to the principle of universality. The organization was not meant to be one of like-minded states. Norway has voted to admit the People's Republic of China to the seat of China. In 1959, Foreign Minister Lange explained Norway's view on the Chinese representation. It is essentially a practical problem. If a government exercises full and effective control over a national territory, it should be recognized under international law. Recognition of a foreign government has never carried with it any moral approval of its actions. The non-recognition of the People's Republic of China as a member state means that its government may justifiably claim that it is not bound by the obligations set forth in the United Nations Charter. What the international community might gain by admitting the People's Republic of China is too often ignored when the representation issue is being discussed.

As a member of the United Nations, the People's Republic of China would not only be pledged to observe the Charter provisions concerning the peaceful settlement of disputes, it would also, by its presence at the United Nations, be engaged in the negotiating machinery which constitutes the practical expression of the Charter provisions for peaceful settlement. In the present situation, the Chinese People's Republic is outside the existing international order and beyond its control.[24]

Rwanda

The representation of China is an important question. The Government of Rwanda supports the principle of a single nation, a single people, and a single China. The Rwanda Government maintains friendly relations with the government of the Republic of China. They regret that a great part of the Chinese people is unable to contribute to peace and international security through the organization.

Since last year, the international situation has completely changed. The world is witnessing a hardening of the position of the People's Republic of China. The conditions which the Peking regime lays down for its admission are totally unacceptable to the Rwanda Government.

Last year, the Peking regime continued to arm a handful of Rwanda refugees so as to restore a feudal monarchy in Rwanda. This is quite paradoxical. The monarchy had been rejected by the overwhelming majority of the people of Rwanda in a referendum conducted under the auspices of the United Nations.

Not so long ago, the same bands of refugees, armed by that same regime created trouble along the national territory frontiers.

Rwanda will not subscribe to a draft resolution which calls for the expulsion of a member state. They believe that the people of Taiwan have the right to choose the regime which suits it and to determine its own destiny.[25]

Sudan

The universality of the United Nations is a necessary condition for its effectiveness. Sudan believes in the absolute necessity of the admission to the United Nations of the People's Republic of China. By this denial of China we are restricting the United Nations. We are hampering it from soaring into wider horizons and more meaningful and fruitful endeavors.[26]

Sweden

Inevitably, in any discussion of the situation in Southeast Asia, one has to remark on the fact that the People's Republic of China is not represented in the United Nations. It cannot be in the interest of the organization that a government that for almost two decades has ruled the mainland of China should not also be allowed to take China's place in the United Nations.[27]

Syria

Syria joins ten other delegations in the call for the discussion of the restoration of its lawful right in the United Nations to the People's Republic of China. Syria has sought to contribute to putting an end to an illegal and abnormal situation. If it continues, it will defeat the purposes of the Charter, and paralyze all endeavors to establish international peace and security.

Here is a great power, the largest of the world in size and population, deprived of its legitimate seat just because another great power considers it not in its interest that the voice of the Chinese be heard in the United Nations. The Charter, since its inception, has allotted China the position of great power, commensurate with its important role in international relations. This position is now greatly enhanced. China is among the nuclear powers. Disarmament, the greatest problem facing the United Nations and the whole of mankind, cannot be achieved without the active participation of this nuclear power.[28]

Thailand

The Thai delegation attaches great importance to the debate on the representation of China in the United Nations. It is not a mere question of procedure or credentials. It raises problems of a political and legal nature which affect our organization, and the peace and security of the entire world.

Friendly relations between the Chinese and the Thais have always existed. When the government of the People's Republic of China was established, relations between the Chinese people and the Thai people drifted apart. They have adopted political principles which are alien to our peaceful way of life.

The government of the Republic of China has settled on the Island which is called Formosa, or Taiwan. It now has diplomatic relations with over half the members of this Assembly. According to the Charter, a member of this organization can only be expelled if, according to Article 6, it has persistently violated the principles contained in the present Charter, and by the General Assembly upon the recommendation of the Security Council. The delegation from Thailand considers that they owe it to their conscience to assert that the government of the Republic of China has not violated the principles of the Charter.[29]

United Kingdom

The necessity for plain speaking is enhanced by the importance and urgency of the question. This is an issue of the utmost concern for Asia, for the United Nations, and for the future of world peace. The British government believes that the seat of China in the United Nations, the seat of a founding member and a permanent member of the Security Council, should be occupied by the Chinese People's Republic. That conviction is firm. It has long been maintained[30]

Union of Soviet Socialist Republics

It is symptomatic that of four states, founding members of the United Nations and permanent members of the Security Council, three of them the Soviet Union, France, and the United Kingdom—favor the restoration of the right of the Chinese People's Republic in the United Nations.

To enhance the role of the United Nations in world affairs, it is necessary to make it a truly international organization. The time is long overdue for restoration of the legitimate rights of the Chinese People's Republic in the United Nations and the expulsion of Chiang Kai-shek's puppets from all its bodies.[31]

FOOTNOTES

[1] Gallup Opinion Index, Report No. 19 (January, 1967) p. 12.

[2] Ibid., pp. 12-15.

[3] George Gallup, "British Voters Do Not See Eye-to-Eye with U. S. Voters on U. N. Seat for Red China," Public Opinion News Service, 5 August, 1953, p. 1.

[4] George Gallup, "Leaders in Education, Religion OK Admitting Red China to U. N.," Public Opinion News Service, 25 May, 1955, p. 1.

[5] George Gallup, "6 out of 10 Support Idea of U. N. Army to Handle 'Trouble Spots', American Institute of Public Opinion, 29 May, 1964, p. 1.

[6] George Gallup, "Public Continues to Oppose U. N. Seat for Communist China", American Institute of Public Opinion, 24 SEptember, 1955, p. 1.

[7] Ibid., p. 2.

[8] George Gallup, "Public Continues to Oppose Red China's Admission to U. N.", American Institute of Public Opinion, 6 October, 1961, p. 1.

[9] George Gallup, "Public Divided on Merits of Sending Food to Red Chinese", American Institute of Public Opinion, 26 June, 1962, p. 1.

[10] Gallup Poll, "Public Seen Willing to Take 'New Look' at Admitting Red China to United Nations", American Institute of Public Opinion, 22 April, 1966, p. 21.

[11] Gallup Political Index, Gallup International Report, No. 17, October, 1966, p. 16.

[12] New York Times, 12 February, 1969, p. 18.

[13] Ibid.

[14] Huot, Sambath, On the Restoration of the Lawful Rights of the People's Republic of China in the United Nations, 18 November, 1966, Permanent Mission of Cambodia to the United Nations, p. 2.

[15] The Honorable Paul Martin, Speech at the Twenty-first Session of the United Nations General Assembly on the Question of Chinese Representation at the United Nations, 23 November, 1966, Canada Press Release.

[16] The Honorable Renan Fuentealba, Speech to the XX General Assembly of the United Nations on the Question of the Admittance of the People's Republic of China to the U. N., 16 November, 1965, p. 3.

[17] The Honorable Mr. Wei Tao-ming, China, Speech, United Nations General Assembly, Twenty-first Session, Provisional Verbatim Record, New York, 18 November, 1966, A/pv 1470, pp. 31-61.

[18] The Honorable Mr. Piccioni, Italy, Speech, United Nations General Assembly, Ibid., pp. 23-25.

[19] H.E. Mr. R. Ramani, Statement on the Restoration of the Lawful Rights of the People's Republic of China in the United Nations to the XXIst Session of the General Assembly, 28 November, 1966, Permanent Mission of Malaysia to the United Nations, p. 2.

[20] The Honorable Mr. Katenga, Malawi, Speech, United Nations General Assembly, Twenty-first Session, Provisional Verbatim Record, New York, 28 November, 1966, A/pv 1480, p. 39.

[21] The Honorable Mangalyn Dugersuren, Mongolia People's Republic, *Statement in the General Debate of the XXI Session of the U. N. General Assembly*, 5 October, 1966, Permanent Mission of the Mongolian People's Republic to the United Nations, p. 16.

[22] H.E. Mr. Khatri, Kingdom of Nepal, *Speech, United Nations General Assembly, op. cit.*, A/pv 1480, pp. 3-11.

[23] H.E. F. H. Corner, *Statement on the Question of the Representation of China made in the Plenary Session of the General Assembly*, 9 November, 1965, Permanent Mission of New Zealand to the United Nations, p. 2.

[24] Jensen, Björn, *Norway in the United Nations* (Oslo: Norwegian Universities Press, 1964) pp. 7-8.

[25] H.E. Mr. Mudenge, Rwanda, Speech, *United Nations General Assembly*, A/pv 1480, *op. cit.*, p. 73.

[26] The Honorable Ibrahim El Moffi, *Statement Delivered at the XXI Session of the General Assembly, United Nations*, 13 October, 1966, Permanent Mission of Sudan to the United Nations, p. 4.

[27] The Honorable Torsten Nilsson, *Statement in the General Debate, United Nations*, 10 October, 1966, Swedish Mission to the United Nations, p. 5.

[28] The Honorable George J. Tomch, Syria, *Speech Made on the Restoration of the Lawful Rights to the People's Republic of China*, United Nations General Assembly, 22 November, 1966, p. 1.

[29] H.E. Visutr Arthayukti, *Statement on Agenda Question 90: Question of the Representation of China in the United Nations*, United Nations, General Assembly, 26 November, 1966, Permanent Mission of Thailand to the United Nations, p. 1.

[30] Lord Caradon, *Statement to the United Nations, General Assembly*, A/pv 1480, *op. cit.*, p. 41.

[31] *Statement by the USSR Delegation in Connection with the Closing of the XXI Session of the U. N. General Assembly*, Press Release No. 51, 21 December, 1966, p. 8.

CHAPTER VII

IMPORTANCE OF RUSSIAN-CHINESE TERRITORIAL DISPUTES TO THE QUESTION

Many people think that a discussion of Chinese territorial claims against Russia is not important to a monograph on Chinese representation in the United Nations. However, public opposition to this representation in the United States, motivated by fear of a gigantic, monolithic Russian-Chinese Communist coalition in the United Nations, makes consideration of Chinese-Russian relations relevant.

In June of 1955, President Eisenhower invited Burmese Prime Minister, U Nu, to Washington. After returning to New York, on 6 July, 1955, U Nu held a press conference at the United Nations. The Burmese statesman had formed an impression that Washington policy-makers did not oppose eventual U. N. admission for Communist China. He thought the problem was timing. Later, U Nu told the Overseas Press Club that Asians did not understand the United States' "fear" of, and "preoccupation" with Communism.[1]

In the United States there still is great fear of Communism. Therefore, there is hostility toward Communist China. If Americans felt that China and Russia were natural rivals in the Far East, as Mr. Attlee of Britain has asserted, then Americans would not be so fearful of China, and might not be so rigid in their attitude against admitting Peking's representative to the U.N.

Chinese territorial claims against Russia are real and valid. It is not suggested that territorial questions are the most important issues in the Chinese-Russian conflict. It is felt, however, that they are of major significance, and are not known or understood by a major section of the American public. Conflicts over land might be more important than questions of ideology.

After the Cuban missile crisis, in 1962, the Chinese taunted Premier Khrushchev for backing down to American power. Mr. Khrushchev replied in a speech to the Supreme Soviet, on 12 December, 1962. He related how the Indians had thrown the Portugese out of Goa, and how Indonesia forced the Dutch out of West Iran. He taunted the Chinese about Macao and Hong Kong. China endured these colonies because it was expedient, or good business for them to do so. Russia did not consider it appeasement for China to continue its concessions to British and Portugese colonialists.

Khrushchev wanted China to settle these questions only when it was in the interest of China and the whole Socialist camp to do so.

In like manner, China should not have attempted to force Russia into ultra-revolutionary acts. During the Cuban crisis, if the Russians had listened to them, the world would have sunk into the morass of a new world war—a thermonuclear war.[2] One month later, the Communist Party of the United States continued the Khrushchev argument. The American Communists stated that their Chinese comrades were applying a double standard. They were not following an adventurous policy in Taiwan, Hong Kong, or Macao. Therefore, they should not advocate adventurism for others.[3]

On 11 August, 1964, Chairman Mao told a delegation of the Japanese Socialist Party that the Kurile Islands must be returned to Japan by Russia and bitterly criticized the Soviet Union for its territorial ambitions. In 1954, when Khrushchev and Bulgarin visited China, Mao took up this question, but the Russians refused to talk about it.

Chairman Mao also said that some people claimed that the Sinkiang area and the territories north of the Amur River must be included in the Soviet Union. According to Mao, the area to the east of Lake Baikal became Russian territory about one hundred years ago. Since then, Vladivostok, Khabarovsk, Kamchatka, and other areas have become Soviet territory. "We have not yet presented our account for this list."[4] These were the exact words of Chairman Mao. The words in quotation marks do not seem very bold. They do, however, speak multitudes. Some day, perhaps in years or perhaps not for decades or centuries, Russian territory in Sinkiang, and in the Vladivostok area, will receive the same treatment as India has received along the McMahon Line, as the Portugese have received in Macao, and stronger treatment than the British have as yet received in Hong Kong.

In Northeastern Asia, the Sino-Soviet boundary arbitrarily cuts across the principal physiographic regions. Starting in the west, the boundary begins at the Afghanistan tri-point on the edge of the Pamirs. The border runs due north from Pereval Beik Pass to the Kizil Jik Dawan Pass.[5] Apparently, the border was established in this region along the water divide. No Chinese government has accepted the Pamir boundary, although the extent of claims has varied.[6] The boundary runs northwesterly through the Tien Shan (Heavenly) Mountains, and across the Ili River. It then proceeds northwest of the Dzungaria Steppes to the Mongolian tri-point in the Altai Mountains.

Western China is divided into two deserts by the Tien Shan Mountains. Those mountains run east-west and extend from the Chinese-Russian border to the southwestern border of the Mongolian People's Republic. The steppes of Dzungaria are north of the Heavenly Mountains. A railroad runs through the Dzungaria Gate along the foot of the Tien Shan Mountains to Urumchi, then eastward to Turfan, Hami, and finally to Peking after a wide, swinging loop south to Lanchow. The Dzungarian Gate is an historic point through which Mongolian invaders traveled on the way to European invasions. Marco Polo did not use it when he went east to China, rather, he used the Wakhan Corridor to the Pamir Plateau, then on to the Court of Kublai Khan, nephew of Genghis Khan, using the Silk Road. The Mongol tribes of Khan traveled through the Dzungarian Gate in the 13th century going in a direction opposite to that of Marco Polo.[7]

Dzungaria is a triangular-shaped basin occupying 270,000 square miles. It has substantial precipitation and can support a large pastoral population. The Muslim Kazakhs in the area have traditionally migrated back and forth from Russian to Chinese territory. Thus, the Russians and Chinese of the area share a common history as well as in the Turkic language. The people have traditionally been lax in practicing Islam. This factor may not be as strong a bond of unity as it would first appear to be.[8]

The large Tarim Basin south of the Heavenly Mountains is the Chinese nuclear-testing area. It is one of the driest regions of Asia. The Altyn Tagh Range of the Himalayas forms the southern boundary of the desert. However, glacier-fed streams descending from the mountains sustain life in widely scattered settlements around this huge wasteland.

East of Mongolia, the frontier region is less complex. For almost its entire length (approximately 2,000 miles), it is a physical boundary which consists of the Amur River and its tributaries, the Argun, and the Ussuri Rivers. From the Mongolian tri-point, the Argun River, by treaty, constitutes the boundary between Chita Oblast (USSR) and the Inner Mongolian Autonomous Region for at least 600 miles. The Great Wall of Genghis Khan cuts diagonally across the border in the area of Manchouli. The Amur forms the boundary for the next 1,000 miles. It flows north and then east and south. There is a great hump in the Chinese territory here. Mostly, the land consists of sparsely settled uplands in the Greater Khingan Range. The Inner Mongolian Autonomous Region is a province of China. The southern boundary in its westerly section is the Great Wall of China. In the vicinity of the Great Khingan hump, the uplands in the west belong to Inner Mongolia, while the eastern lowlands from Harbin to the Ussuri constitute the fertile plains of northern Manchuria. The Chinese Eastern Railway crosses the Sungari River at Harbin on its way to Vladivostok. The Southern Manchurian Railway runs south from Harbin to Mukden, Anshan, Dairen, and Port Arthur. The location of the Chinese Eastern Railroad demonstrates the exposed position of the Russian Trans-Ussuri Territory. The natural hinterland of Vladivostok, the "fortress of the East," is not the Amur Valley to the north, but the provinces of Manchuria to the northwest.[10]

East of Khingan, the frontier region is a low land—the Amur-Ussuri Plain. Elevations are relatively low, and the area is generally poorly drained, rolling country. The large area of forest has been an economic attraction to the Chinese. Along the Amur, there are excellent stands of pine, larch, cedar, and spruce.[11] At the City of Khabarovsk, there is a confluence of the Amur and the Ussuri. Here the Ussuri forms the border on a north-south axis. The Amur departs from its easterly course and heads northeast to Siberia and the Sea of Okhotsk. Along the Ussuri River there are also excellent stands of timber. These occupy swampy areas where hard woods prevail, particularly oak and maple. This northern area of Manchuria has great development potential. Good utilization of this valuable area has probably suffered, because it has been isolated from both the Soviet and the Chinese centers of production and communications.[12] The Ussuri River, on a north-south axis, constitutes the main boundary between the Primorsky Kray of the USSR and the Southern Manchurian Section of the Chinese People's Republic. The area of Southern Manchuria was extensively developed by the Japanese. It has a broadly diversified manufacturing base, producing thirty per cent of China's coal, at least seventy per cent of its power, and half of its electric power. Accordingly, it has often been called the "Ruhr of the Far East."[13] Is it any wonder that the Chinese were anxious when General MacArthur approached the Yalu? The Russians had just recently pulled out of Manchuria. They had taken practically all that was worthwhile with them.[14] The Chinese had been able to make a fresh start, but only a limited one, when the Korean War started. They did not want the Americans to disrupt the little rebuilding which had been accomplished.

The Soviet population of the Far-Eastern borderlands probably totals little more than four million. There is a weak industrial base, and little agricultural development. The population clings to the Trans-Siberian Railway. It would not be altogether wrong to characterize the populace as members of a Far-Eastern Soviet garrison. Essentially, the Soviet Far East is a strategic area, more important to Russia as an outpost on the Pacific, than as a section economically united to the rest of the USSR.

At the junction of the Ussuri and the Songacha Rivers, the boundary proceeds up the latter to Lake Khanka. A minor water divide forms the border southwestward from the Lake. Then, the frontier is a straight line south-southeastward across the Sui-fen Lowland. After the boundary crosses the Sui-fen River, it is delineated by the Ta-wu-she-Ho, a southbank tributary. The boundary proceeds southward to the drainage divide of the coastal range. The Korean tri-point is situated on the Tumen River about ten miles above the estuary.[15] The Yalu River forms the boundary between North Korea and China.

Soviet Central Asia and the Sinkiang-Uigur Autonomous Region once formed the ancient Turkestan Empire. The Russian-Chinese boundary in this area has been unchanged for almost a century. Before and after the Bolshevik Revolution, the Russians have crossed the border for political or economic advantage.[17] Historically, the Central Asian frontier had been occupied by numerous, fragmented tribes and peoples. China developed with an economy based upon irrigated rice culture far to the east in the great river basins. The steppes and deserts of Central

Asia were ill-suited to Chinese settlement. Czarist Russia, essentially a European power, was occupied in creating a western-oriented nation-state. This area could not be ignored. Power politics required that it be controlled. Politics, too, abhors a vacuum. If the respective areas were not policed, then one side or the other would end up with a strategic advantage.[17] During the Manchu era, in the early 18th century, Chinese influence extended west to Lake Balkhash. This was not far from the Aral Sea. During the early part of the 19th century, the vigor of the Manchu Dynasty waned. It became less able to resist the pressures placed upon it by foreign states. Russia was the equal of the other European nations; probably worse, because Russia took more territory.

Russia began in this period a southward movement into Turkestan from the earlier east-west line of penetration into Siberia. Czarist forces brought Russia into direct contact with the Manchu administration in Turkestan.[18] As China became weaker, Russia forced more and more concessions from the Chinese. The 1860 Treaty of Peking created a Manchu-Russian boundary which recognized the de facto Russian territorial conquests up to that date. Between 1860 and 1895, Russia penetrated further into Sinkiang, through the Ili River Valley. The presence of British troops in the Indian sub-continent, and of the British fleet beyond, guaranteed the stability of the 1860 Pamir boundaries.[19] The Chinese could not by themselves contain or control the Russian influence. Russian expansion into Turkestan alarmed the British and led to bilateral agreements defining their respective spheres of influence.

Even at Yalta, a half-century later, Churchill and Stalin were still deciding spheres of influence. Churchill admitted to having set down on a piece of scrap paper the settlement of affairs in the Balkans. The lives of millions of peoples depended on this bit of scrap-paper work. Churchill must have been uneasy about the offhand manner in which the fate of millions had been decided and wanted to burn the paper. Stalin told him to keep the paper and not to burn it. Stalin evidently was so satisfied with his sphere of influence that he did not care about treating millions in such debonair fashion.[20]

In 1895, a British-Russian bilateral agreement created the Wakhan Corridor as an Afghan barrier between Russian-Turkestan, and British-India. This strange-looking feature on a map is a tribute to British diplomatic genius. It was an adequate solution to a potentially serious problem. The Chinese Communists dropped claims to sections of it in 1953.[21]

Russia penetrated to the Pacific area and established its sphere of influence there, because it was the path of least resistance. Expansion was blocked in Europe. Furthermore, Siberia was appealing. It had natural wealth, furs, timber, and minerals. The rate of Russian expansion into Siberia was amazing. In 1580, Perm, just west of the Urals, was the eastern limit of Russian penetration. Within two generations, Russian cities were established at Tomsk, on the Ob; at Yeniseysk, on the Yenisey; at Yakutsk, on the Lena; and Okhotsk, on the Pacific. This last city was established in 1638. It was located at latitude 60°N., while Peking was at 40°N. This line of city forts, anchored on the Pacific, was well north of China or Chinese-suzerain territory. Okhotsk was more than 1,000 miles north of the Yalu. The northern territory was cold, barren, and isolated. It is easy to see how the Russians had this territory to themselves. During the last party of the 17th century, Russian explorers moved down into the Amur Valley. The Manchu Dynasty was then at the height of its power.

Manchu China defeated Russia. The Russians were forced to withdraw from the middle and lower Amur Valley by the terms of the Nerchinsk Treaty in 1689. Under this treaty, Russia received compensating territory elsewhere—90,000 square miles of territory, even though China had been the victor.[22]

After that, the Kiakhta Treaty of Peace in 1727 gained Russia more territory. About 40,000 square miles in the Lake Baikal area were ceded by China. This Treaty remained in force until 1858. Then came the Treaty of Aigun, and the Treaty of Peking in 1860. These treaties brought the boundary to the Amur, as far east as the Ussuri with one exception. The "Manchu" settlers, situated on the north bank of the Amur between the Zela River and the village of Holdazin, would remain under Manchu administration. The "Manchu" settlers in these so-called '64 villages' were guaranteed their domiciles in perpetuity. During the Boxer Rebellion, Russia expelled the "Manchu" inhabitants and assumed jurisdiction of the territory.[23]

Current border disputes between China and Russia have taken place in the area of the Ussuri River. This is a particularly sensitive area to the Chinese, because of duress under which the Treaty of Peking was signed in 1860. Current disputes are only an indication of bigger conflicts to come.

The Peking Agreement supplemented the Aigun Treaty, and it completed the delineation of the frontier in this area. Russia gained the harbor of Vladivostok and 130,000 square miles of territory bounded by the Amur, Ussuri, and Tumen Rivers and the Sea of Japan.[24] The Treaty of Peking also specified that in Turkestan the boundary should be the existing line of Chinese pickets. Thus, Russia gained what it had conquered up to the Chinese defense line. In 1871, there was a Moslem revolt against the Manchu Dynasty in the Ili Valley of Turkestan. The Russians occupied the valley, ostensibly to keep order.[25] China could not force the Russians out. Finally, in the 1880's, protocols signed at Kashgar and Ili delimited and demarcated the boundary between Russia and Chinese Turkestan as far south as Kizil Jik Dawan Pass.[26]

In 1895, the British entered the area and helped to restrain Russian Imperialism. The Russians and British decided border problems without consulting the

Chinese. The Chinese maintain that they did not recognize the boundaries as settled. However, the 1953 Communist-Chinese Atlas withdraws Chinese territorial claims from the Wakhan Corridor of Afghanistan.[27]

In 1911, during the chaotic period of the Manchu collapse, the Tsitsihar Treaty was signed. The Tsitsihar frontier generally encroached about five miles into China along a sixty-mile front. Neither the Government of the Republic of China, nor the Communist regime has recognized the validity of this agreement. Lenin repeatedly promised to restore this territory. Moreover, after the Russian Revolution in 1919, the Soviet Government announced an intention to abrogate all agressive Czarist treaties signed with China after 1896. Soviet maps still, however, adhere to the Tsitsihar Treaty.

In 1951, the respective Communist governments signed agreements on navigation and construction on border waterways of the Amur, Ussuri, Argun, and Songacha Rivers, and Lake Khanka. The Treaty states that the traffic in the rivers will follow the main navigational channels, regardless of their relationship to the state frontier. This wording strongly implies that the state frontier is not directly related to the Thalweg, i.e. the main navigable channel.[28] This problem is central to the incidentals of the current dispute. The big issue, however, is the entire Russian Far Eastern outpost.

In the 19th century, Russia pushed south to warmer Pacific water and took the maritime provinces between the Amur and Ussuri Rivers, and the sea. Just as the political hawks in the U. S. Congress were crying about the manifest destiny of the United States, and the need to spread the United States to the Pacific Ocean, the Russians were winning the battle of the east and gaining their frontier on the Pacific.

The 1911 Agreement at Tsitsihar redefined the border between Mongolia and the Argun, ceding approximately 375 square miles to Russia. Japan had been seizing Chinese territory since 1895, when the Pescadores and Formosa were taken. Japan had a splendid little war with China, just as the United States, a few years later, had its "splendid little war" with Spain. Japan wanted Port Arthur, but this was denied to her by the combined efforts of Russia, Germany, and France. Now Russia, posing as China's friend, gained for itself, by intrigue, what Japan had won by war, but had subsequently deprived of by European powers. Russia secured permission to build a railway across Manchuria and also obtained leases to Port Arthur and Dairen. Russia could not digest her gains. She was disrupted by revolution, and could not supply her Far-Eastern forces. Japan became dominant in the area.

In the period immediately following the Bolshevik Revolution, the Soviet leaders were inclined to disassociate themselves from Czarist imperial policies. Russian weakness encouraged Japan to intervene. Attempts were made to establish anti-Soviet governments from time to time across the vast stretch of Siberia.

During 1919, the situation gradually worsened for the Bolshevik opposition in Siberia. Finally, a compromise Far-East Republic came into existence in 1920. It was supposed to be neutral. Japan withdrew, and Russia outmaneuvered her by skillful diplomacy. In 1922, the neutral republic was voted into the Russian Soviet Federated Socialist Republic. Once again, Russian authority extended over Siberia to the Pacific. Now Russia engaged in a classic case of double-cross and duplicity. The Soviets reneged on their promise to sell the Chinese Eastern Railway to China. The railway was sold to archenemy Japan in 1935. This reflected the power situation in the early 1930's. Japan had invaded Manchuria in 1931, and had established the puppet state of Manchukuo.

During the later stages of World War II, it was generally believed that the war with Japan in the Far East would go on for many months after the cessation of European hostilities, and cost many American lives. Thus, U. S. military strategists were eager to have Soviet participation, with a view to bringing the Pacific War to an early close. At about this time, Prime Minister Churchill was desperately eager to have the British Fleet take part in the Pacific Naval War. Admiral King did not want the British Fleet and in spite of Churchill's pleas, the United States Navy did not want British assistance. To further add insult to this injury, it was alleged by American Naval Officers that British ships could not keep up with the American Fast Carrier Task Forces. General Lord Ismay, Churchill's Chief of Staff, wrote humorously of this in his memoirs. At the Second Quebec Conference, Churchill requested that the British Fleet be sent to the Central Pacific after the defeat of Germany to operate under United States Command. Admiral King opposed this intrusion of the British into his own pet war. When President Roosevelt approved this request of the "Former Naval Person," it was jokingly said by Lord Ismay that Admiral King went into a swoon. The British Fleet did not have a vast impact on the Naval War against Japan, nor did the Russian Armed Forces contribute much to the war against Japan. However, the Russians did obtain substantial territory and hegemony for a week of war against Japan.

An adviser to President Kennedy criticized the State Department in 1961 because it still thought in terms of a "Sino-Soviet bloc." Tactically Russia and China may be allies, but only for a short period. Chinese outrage over lost territory will not permit a permanent alliance. Theoretically international Communism is not concerned with border problems. Therefore, in theory, border problems are not vital ones. However, land comes before ideology. Even if there were no ideological conflict between Russian and Chinese Communism, there would be the question of lost territory. The Chinese can never admit that sections of their territory, now controlled by Russia, are not truly Chinese. To do so would be shameful, a "loss of face." As Chairman Mao has stated, an accounting for territory lost to Russia has not yet been made. An accounting has been demanded in the case of Formosa. Chinese insistence on this issue is well-known.

Russian attempts to extend its territory have been imperialistic. After World War II, Russia acquired part of East Prussia, including Königsberg, as well as the Baltic States, Estonia, Latvia and Lithuania. Eastern Poland was seized, and the Poles were told to take compensating territory from Germany. In 1945, Sub-Carpathian Ruthenia was acquired from Czechoslovakia. Strong pressure was put on Turkey for territorial concessions, and for bases on the Straits. These last endeavors failed, but, since August, 1939, the effective boundaries of Soviet power have shifted about 750 miles to the west and 600 miles to the southwest.

In Asia, the negotiations for Russia's entry into the war against Japan had the effect of allowing Russia to regain the territory lost at Portsmouth, New Hampshire. President Theodore Roosevelt was active in negotiating the end of the Russian-Japanese War of 1904-05. Four decades later, a President Franklin Roosevelt agreed to give Soviet Russia much territory lost by the Czars to Japan at Portsmouth. Port Arthur became a Soviet Naval Base. Chiang Kai-shek was forced to acquiesce in the establishment of a Soviet satellite in Outer Mongolia. During the 1930's, Russian influence in Sinkiang had been dominant. It was relaxed during the war, but gradually reasserted after 1946. The industrial wealth in the former Japanese puppet state of Manchukuo was stolen by the Soviets and shipped to European Russia.

Stalin had the limited mind of a stubborn Georgian peasant. His policy was to exploit ruthlessly the greatly increased military power of the Soviet Union, but to withdraw at any serious threat of a major war. So abusive was Stalin that Tito, a loyal Socialist, was forced out of the Russian sphere of influence. Stalin expanded and fortified the Soviet position whenever possible and never volunteered to let go of anything once held. However, Soviet policy succeeded only where backed by overwhelming Soviet power. Stalin, by his force and grossness, made things simple for the West; they fought him on every issue. The unfortunate thing was that Secretary of State, John Foster Dulles, came to power just after Stalin died and kept on fighting Stalin instead of shifting weapons and tactics. No deal could be made with Stalin, but a quiet, firm man could handle Premier Khrushchev. A young American President combined the use of power with restraint and handled Mr. Khrushchev in masterly fashion during the Cuban missile crisis.

When Tito had used his courage and prestige to resist Stalin, the answer from the Georgian peasant was abuse, but no action. This lesson was not lost on the other Communist leaders in Eastern Europe nor on Chairman Mao. Mao resisted Khrushchev revisionism, rather than Stalinism, but he did make the break. It has been said by some observers that Mao cannot forgive the Russians for polluting international Communism with capitalistic thinking. Conversely, Moscow cannot forgive Peking for cracking the solidarity of the worldwide Communist movement. It is also important that China cannot forget lost territory, and Russia may fear what may be coming on that issue.

The establishment of a Chinese-Communist regime in Peking marked the beginning of a new era in Asia, and one which would have far-reaching implications for the entire world. Professor Reischauer, of Harvard, may belittle the industrial capabilities of China and underrate the potential of China. It seems that the professor does not consider ideology to be too serious, but it is a key issue. Ideology is of supreme importance to Mao. Professor Tang expresses this view repeatedly, and warns that we should not underrate the People's Republic of China. The Communist success in China brought to an end foreign overseas intervention in Chinese affairs. The Soviets, too, have been compelled to reassess their strategy in Asia. Hitherto, Russian expansion in East and Inner Asia, whether Tsarist or Soviet, had occurred mainly at the expense of a weak and disorganized China. The very weakness of China invited and encouraged the expansion of Russia, as well as the imperial rivalry of Japan, Germany, France, and Great Britain. Russian Imperialism was just as bad as or worse than that of her European neighbors.

Russian national interest demanded territory from China. When Russia was able to extract concessions from China, it did so. The unequal treaties are ample proof of this policy. There are many who claim that treaties signed under duress are not valid and binding. Hitler claimed this about Versailles. Will future generations of Red Guards consider the Russian-Chinese borders as historical, or as determined by unequal treaties signed under duress? A landlord will not rest until he receives fair rent for his property. It seems that the Chinese will not rest while parts of their ancient domain are under the suzerainty of a foreigner.

In Central Asia, a section north of the Afghanistan tri-point has not been demarcated and is, therefore, "in dispute." Territory from the Mongolian tri-point to the Argun River, in the vicinity of the Genghis Khan Great Wall, is disputed by the question of the validity of the 1911 Tsitsihar Treaty. All Chinese governments have declared this agreement invalid. In the Argun, Amur, and Ussuri Rivers, agreements indicate that the parties are sidestepping the issue of a boundary line. But the issue is not being sidestepped in 1969. The agreements emphasize navigational rights, but do not establish a boundary. Therefore, in the river areas, the boundaries should be considered indefinite. The area of the "64 villages" should be regarded as disputed. People given land in perpetuity were evicted in two generations.

On a short-term basis, the People's Government of China seems to have acquiesced in the de facto border. The 1953 Communist maps have dropped claims to sections of the Pamirs in the Tadzhik Soviet Socialist Republic. Perhaps China is looking at long-term reconciliation. When we contemplate strategy, we think of meeting the enemy in combat under advantageous conditions. That is the key here. Meet the enemy when you have the advantage. China is now inferior militarily to Russia. It will remain so indefinitely. So, China may allow the matter to rest for the time being. However, the history of unequal treaties will be passed along to new generations. Chinese territorial claims against Russia will pass from generation to generation. The feud will live like Balkan feuds, simmering and always ready to come to the surface. The Chinese want to rectify the borders, which are a monstrous product of former wrongs and shames. Versailles was a strong tool in the hands of Hitler, and Russian Imperialism in Asia will be a strong tool in the hands of Chinese leaders in ages to come.

Immediately after coming to power, the Chinese-Communist Regime took a number of steps to organize and integrate both Sinkiang and Manchuria. Soviet control, which had lingered on since World War II, was greatly reduced and finally liquidated. It seems that Sinkiang and Manchuria have become truly oriented toward China despite minor ethnic problems.[29]

Russia seems to have a guilty conscience about Siberia. During June, 1966, President Nikolai V. Podgorny warned in Khabarovsk that the Soviet people were alert and determined to protect their Far-Eastern territories from invaders. The Order of Lenin was awarded to the territory. Two weeks earlier, Leonid I. Brezhnev, the Communist Party Chief, had flown to Vladivostok to honor that territory also with the Order of Lenin.[30] These awards seem like morale boosters to frontier defenders. In November of 1966, the U.S.S.R. embassy sharply denied a *New York Times* report dealing with Russian-Chinese border clashes.[31] Foreign Minister Andrei A. Gromyko, in talks with United States officials, stressed his nation's concern with China's growing arsenal of nuclear weapons. Mr. Gromyko supposedly made clear that the break with China was quite fundamental.[32] This *New York Times* statement was later angrily denied by the Russians, but there is usually more than a hint of truth when the *New York Times* makes such statements and interpretations. Many *New York Times* articles after the Cuban missile crisis of 1962 hinted that Khrushchev was to be eased out of power.

Socialist solidarity is a myth; the Sino-Soviet conflict is not a gigantic hoax. Soviet economist V. Lan, writing in the latest issue of the authoritative Soviet Magazine, *Mirovava Economika i Mezhdunarodnive Otnosheniva*, sharply chided his fellow Soviet economists. Those men who predicted disaster for the American economy were wrong. The Communist challenge produced changes in the United States which virtually guaranteed that the United States of America would never again have a depression like the one which began in 1929. Therefore, Soviet economists will have to face the realities of American capitalism. Real wages of American workers have risen substantially since 1945.[33] This praise and admiration for consumer capitalism came from Russia. The Chinese hate it and call it "Khrushchev Revisionism."

In April of 1966, China announced sweeping new controls of river-boat traffic, and of the use of frontier ports and streams which will primarily affect Soviet ships. New regulations to safeguard China's national sovereignty will affect Soviet vessels operating between Siberian and Northeastern Chinese points. Much of the Argun, and all of the Amur frontier, are undefined on Chinese maps published as recently as 1965. These rules, also, affect traffic on the Sungari. Essentially, the rules are nuisances—regulations on dumping, flying the Chinese flag, cargo, signal flags, and port procedures. It seems to be a matter of principle and simple assertion of control and an indication of things to come. Wounded pride and memories of exploitation linger.

Ever since the English colonized North America, Russia had been colonizing Chinese territory in Asia.

The Russian Empire spread to its present Asian frontiers on the Amur-Argun area, and in Far Turkestan, less than two hundred years ago. China reached those frontiers two thousand or more years ago. Since then, China has advanced or receded from them in periods of rise and decline. While advancing over the nomadic lands of Asia, during roughly the same period as the United States took Texas and California from Mexico and the Indians, the Russians followed a policy of nonalignment with the sea powers. Russia reached the Pacific by a process of attrition. The Russians avoided a head-on clash with China, while encouraging her conflicts with invaders from the sea. If the United States would allow her, China would focus attention on her natural rival to the north.

Despite occasional unconfirmed reports of border clashes between China and the Soviet Union, the shooting incidents along the Ussuri River on 2 March, 1969, marked the first time that either government reported an armed incident. These incidents surely indicate that the Soviet-Chinese territorial issues are vital. The Soviet Far-Eastern region was seized from China by the Czars in the late 19th century through a series of unequal treaties. China is seeking to detach 500,000 square miles of territory from the Soviet Far-Eastern maritime provinces. Western intelligence analysts know that the threat of Chinese attack in the disputed border regions has a high priority in Soviet defense planning. Soviet troop strength in the Warsaw Pact area has not yet been significantly diminished by the build-up in the Far East. But the quality of Soviet forces in Europe is believed to have suffered.[34]

Even now, however, some analysts dismiss the territorial issue as a minor one which can be turned off as the political climate dictates. This seems like weak thinking since men are being killed by each side along the border.

It has been about a year since the first clashes on the Ussuri River. In the spring of 1969 that fighting captured wide attention. The world was treated to a lesson of history—land is more important than ideology. Some observers believed that China had provoked the incidents in order to spur national unity after the turmoil of the cultural revolution. Others placed the blame on Moscow. They argued that if the Soviet Union could brutally invade Czechoslovakia, it could also provoke war against Peking.

Fortunately, war has not come, but there has not been much progress in the negotiations. Clashes again took place in the late spring and summer of 1969. The August clash, in the northern areas of Sinkiang along the central Asian border, involved fighting and negotiating at the same time. While a border pact was being negotiated to settle some of the problems along the Ussuri River, new clashes were breaking out in central Asia. Some observers have charged that the Soviet aim in Asia is to set up a free Sinkiang. Peking has repeatedly charged that the Soviets have collaborated with Turkestan leaders who have fled Sinkiang.

Soviet Premier Kosygin visited Chou En-lai in September, 1969. As a result of their meeting, an agreement was made to discuss the border disputes. Perhaps the Chinese feared an Asian–Czechoslovakia-style invasion. Regardless of the reasons, talks did take place in October, 1969. The Chinese appear to be not erratic, but rational men, ready to back off and at least discuss the issues.

Statements from Peking and Moscow before the October, 1969, talks indicated that both sides simply wanted to improve relations. The Chinese seemed to be afraid that if they did not at least talk, they perhaps would be subject to a preemptive attack which could wipe out their nuclear installations. The question of actual territory seems to be irreconcilable. The Chinese have maintained that the old treaties which China signed with Czarist Russia were unequal and unjust. It is almost impossible for the Russians to give satisfaction on this score. How could a Soviet Government repudiate treaties and return land which has been Russian for a century?

The talks have continued into the spring of 1970. Evidently, no real progress has been made. Nothing concrete has been done, and recently each side has stepped up its propaganda effort against the other.

What should the United States do? This country should not directly take advantage of the situation, but could look back to John Quincy Adams for an answer. Rather than interfere in the affairs of other nations, as Henry Clay wanted us to interfere in Latin America during the 1820's, American should follow the noble high road. We should be what John Quincy Adams wanted us to be—a noble example to others, and back off a little from the exercise of our enormous power.

The Warsaw talks between the United States and Peking will be renewed. President Nixon seems to be taking the correct approach. He is trying for a practical improvement in relations without dramatic gestures which might invite dramatic rebuffs. The sad thing is that we still cannot talk at the United Nations.

FOOTNOTES

[1] Facts on File, Vol. XV, 1955, p. 224.
[2] Doolin, Dennis J., *Territorial Claims in the Sino-Soviet Conflict,* Hoover Institution Studies: 7 (Stanford: The Hoover Institution on War, Revolution and Peace, 1965), p. 28.
[3] *Ibid.,* p. 29.
[4] *Ibid.,* p. 44.

[5]The Geographer. Office of Research in Economics and Science. *International Boundary Study, No. 64: China-USSR Boundary*, Department of State, United States of America, 14 February, 1966, p. 1.

[6]*Ibid.*, p. 5.

[7]*Ibid.*, p. 9.

[8]Jackson, W. A. Douglas, *Russo-Chinese Borderlands* (New York: D. VanNostrand Company, Inc., 1962) p. 11.

[9]*Ibid.*, p. 7.

[10]*Ibid.*, p. 21.

[11]Geographer, U. S. Dept. of State, *op. cit., p. 3.*

[12]*Ibid.*, p. 3.

[13]Jackson, *op. cit.*, p. 18.

[14]Tang, Peter S. H., Lectures, Boston College, *op. cit.*

[15]Geographer, U. S. Dept. of State, *op. cit.*, p. 8.

[16]Jackson, *op. cit.*, p. 3.

[17]Geographer, U. S. Dept. of State, *op. cit.*, p. 3.

[18]*Ibid.*, p. 4.

[19]Jackson, *op. cit.*, p. 3.

[20]Churchill, Winston S., *Triumph and Tragedy* (Boston: Houghton Mifflin Company, 1953) p. 228.

[21]Geographer, U. S. Dept. of State, *op. cit.* Map preceding page 1.

[22]Geographer, U. S. Dept. of State, *op. cit.*, p. 8.

[23]*Ibid.*, p. 10.

[24]*Ibid.*, p. 10.

[25]*Ibid.*, p. 11.

[26]*Ibid.*, p. 12.

[27]*Ibid.*, p. 13.

[28]*Ibid.*, p. 13.

[29]Snow, Edgar, *The Other Side of the River* (New York: Random House, Inc., 1961) p. 647.

[30]Anderson, Raymond, *The New York Times*, 2 June, 1966, p. 21.

[31]*New York Times*, 29 November, 1966, p. 30.

[32]Beecher, William, *New York Times*, 22 November, 1966, p. 1.

[33]Doolin, Dennis J., *op., cit.*, p. 51.

[34]*New York Times*, 3 March, 1969, p. 1.

CHAPTER VIII

SOME SOLUTIONS AND THEIR MERIT

There have been many variations of the two-China theme. No one of them has value, because no one will work. No Chinese government will accept the idea of anything except one China. A favorite story of Abraham Lincoln illustrates the Chinese position. Lincoln asked a person how many legs a dog would have if the dog's tail were called a leg. The person answered "five." Lincoln replied: "No, calling a tail a leg don't make it a leg." There is only one China. Talking of two Chinas does not mean two exist.

Policy Panel Report, United Nations Association of America

This panel included Lucian W. Pye, of M.I.T.; Arthur Dean, a partner in Mr Dulles' old firm, Sullivan and Cromwell; and Joseph E. Johnson, of the Carnegie Endowment for International Peace. There were other distinguished private and public servants in this group, under the Chairmanship of Robert V. Roosa, of Brown Brothers, Harriman & Company.

The panel believed that the time had come (in October of 1966) for the United States to support some form of two-China solution to the representation question in the United Nations. It was assumed that Peking would at first reject the offer, even if it included the possibility of a seat in the Security Council, but that ultimately Peking would modify that policy in order to bring it into accord with present-day realities. The panel did not believe that the United States should support any change in Chinese representation in the Security Council, unless Taiwan's membership in the Assembly were maintained.[1]

This report was satisfactory as far as it went. It did not go far enough. Peking will not accept it. The Chinese see the outside world as either openly hostile covertly opposed, or jealous of China's rise. The Chinese Communists remain convinced that their new way is as superior to all competing ways as they were formerly convinced that the Confucian Empire was superior to the barbarians Chinese policy will seek to avoid a settlement which would leave her in the second rank of powers. The Chinese believe that supreme power is their heritage, and that any inferior status is but the prelude to further decline.[2]

It would be degrading for two Chinese governments to be members of the United Nations. The People's Republic of China in the U. N. along with the Republic of China imply equal status for these two governments. Peking's pride will never tolerate such implied equality, even if Peking has the permanent seat on the Security Council. Peking will, at least, insist upon as many seats as Russia. To save face and also to keep the people of Taiwan represented, there must be additional General Assembly seats for Manchuria, Sinkiang, and Tibet.

Fifth Hammarskjöld Forum

The Bar Association of the City of New York has conducted forums for seven years on "The Role of Law in the Settlement of International Disputes." These forums have attempted to show that only by substituting the rule of law may war be eliminated as the ultimate means of settling international disputes.

The forum attempted to answer the question: "Is it possible to have world peace through world law while leaving outside the present treaty structure the giant nation—China—containing one-fourth of the human race?" Can there really be a solution to humanity's dilemma without China's participation? China has sat in on no disarmament conferences. It has no representation in the United Nations. Yet its actions and its expressed views impair the effectiveness of international agreements reached without its participation.

The Fifth Hammarskjöld Forum of 2 December, 1963, concluded with three possible changes in the representation of China in the United Nations. One would substitute Communist China for Nationalist China. This would be strictly a new-membership situation, not a matter of credentials. But it would not work. Under Article 4(2) of the Charter, new members must be recommended by the Security Council. There could be a veto by Nationalist China. If not, there would always be the threat of a veto by the United States.

A second alternative suggested representation of both Communist China and Nationalist China in the United Nations. This can be made to work legally, but it is of no value since both Communist and Nationalist China oppose it.

Finally, the Forum suggested a possible amendment with respect to China's seat in the Security Council. This amendment would reduce by one the number of members of the Security Council possessing a veto. Under Article 108, amendments to the Charter require approval by two-thirds of the members of the United Nations, including all the permanent members of the Security Council. Nationalist China would probably veto such an amendment. Even if there were no vote, the People's Republic of China would never accept it. This would be an unthinkable indignity to impose upon Peking. Chinese honor would not permit membership under such conditions of humiliation.

Implementation of the Cairo Agreement of December, 1943

Certain scholars have proposed that Formosa should be returned to China to implement the 1943 Cairo Agreement. This does not seem to be a valid argument. Although Britain denies that Formosa was in fact legally returned to China after World War II, other nations disagree, even though the Japanese Peace Treaty was not signed until 1951. The British hold that the sovereignty of Formosa is in legal limbo. However, the Republic of China exercised de facto sovereignty over Formosa for four years before the People's Republic of China won the Civil War on mainland China in 1949. No consensus had been reached among the allied powers by 1951. Therefore, the Japanese Peace Treaty of that year stated simply that Japan renounced all right, title and claim to Formosa and the Pescadores. The Peace Treaty was signed two years after the People's Republic of China was proclaimed. De jure sovereignty is denied by de facto possession.

The principle of international law, *rebus sic stantibus*, can be applied to nullify the Cairo Declaration, signed in December, 1943, by the United States, the United Kingdom, and the Republic of China. Under the principle *rebus sic stantibus* (with things remaining thus), treaties are binding and remain the same only as long as the relevant facts and circumstances remain the same. At Cairo, the government of the Republic of China, was promised that Japan would return Formosa to China. To implement that agreement by action now would be to create a theoretical absurdity, to deny The Republic of China its very existence. We do not keep a promise to a government, when, to keep that promise, we have to take away the existence of the government to which the promise was originally made. A distinction must be made between the Chinese nation and the Republic of China. President Roosevelt wanted the Chinese nation to be represented in the United Nations as a great power. However, at Cairo, Roosevelt and Churchill made a promise, not to the Chinese people, but to the government of the Republic of China.

FOOTNOTES

[1] United Nations Association of the United States of America. *China, The United Nations and United States Policy* (New York: 1966) p. 40.

[2] Fitzgerald, C. P., *The Chinese View of Their Place in the World*, Chatham House Essays Royal Institute of International Affairs (London: Oxford University Press, 1966) p. 68.

CHAPTER IX

A SOLUTION
ARGUMENT IN THE AFFIRMATIVE

At a recent meeting of the American Historical Association in New York, Professor Fairbank referred to a Chinese proverb which implies that a man who knows his adversary and himself will eventually have success. Let us then be ready for the next initiative from Peking. We can expect that any initiative from China will be based on, among other factors, the five principles of peaceful coexistence, as stated in the Bandung Conference of April, 1955. Those principles were:

(1) Mutual respect for each other's territorial integrity
(2) Mutual respect for sovereignty
(3) Mutual nonaggression
(4) Equality and mutual benefit
(5) Peaceful coexistence

In addition to these, the Chinese Communist Premier made the following demands. Supposedly these would have to be satisfied before Peking would agree to enter the United Nations:

1. The expulsion of the Republic of China from the United Nations.
2. The complete reorganization of the Organization. Reorganization would include the expulsion of Imperialist Puppets.
3. The withdrawal of the General Assembly Resolution condemning Peking as an aggressor in the Korean conflict.
4. The branding of the United States as an aggressor in that conflict.

Obviously, these are unacceptable conditions to the United States. Not all of them can be seriously considered. According to these terms, the United States itself would have to leave the organization.

The Charter will not be changed. The United States will not be branded as the aggressor in Korea, and the United States will not be expelled from the U. N. Perhaps China will not insist upon complete satisfaction of these demands. If Chinese honor is saved, there may be a way to reach an accommodation. Chairman Mao has said: "In this world, things are complicated and are decided by many factors. We should look at problems from different aspects, not from just one."[1]

The flag of the People's Republic of China gives a clue to a possible solution. It is a red flag with five stars. China could have one permanent seat on the Security Council and five seats in the General Assembly. The Peking government could be

83

acknowledged by the U. N. Credentials Committee to be the government of China. Since China has almost eight hundred million people, this fact could be acknowledged in General Assembly representation. After World War II, Russia demanded three General Assembly seats, because there were many members of the British Commonwealth having individual seats in the General Assembly. The United States perhaps did not demand additional seats because, with the Federal character of our government, no way could be found to distribute more than one General Assembly seat to the United States of America. The United States could not have demanded forty-eight seats.

It would be a great boost for Chinese pride to have five seats. In a way, it would be justice, as well. The Soviet Union and the United States between them have about four hundred million people. Russia has three seats in the General Assembly. Russia and America have between them four seats in the General Assembly and two permanent seats on the Security Council. Since China has almost twice the combined population of these two countries, it would not be untoward if China had one more seat than these two powers combined in the General Assembly. Many nations, particularly India, might demand such representation themselves. However, India is not a nuclear power. India and those of similar mind might be so pleased to have China within the U. N. family that they would acquiesce in additional seats for China.

The General Assembly Chinese seats could be distributed as follows:

1. China-Peking government (also having a permanent seat on the Security Council).
2. Inner Mongolia. This autonomous region was organized by the People's Republic on 12 May, 1947. Its boundaries could include Manchuria.
3. Sinkiang. This new dominion in Central Asia is China's richest region in strategic materials. It comprises Chinese Turkestan, Kulia, and Kashgaria.
4. Tibet. Under a pact signed on 23 May, 1951, Tibet accepted the suzerainty of the People's Republic. The Dalai Lama was demoted in December of 1964. Revolts continued in 1965 and 1966. In 1961, the International Commission of Jurists at Geneva charged the Communist regime with genocide in Tibet. A General Assembly seat for Tibet under Chinese suzerainty might lead the way to peace in the area.
5. Formosa. A General Assembly seat would be allocated to the Nationalist representative from Taiwan. Peking would oppose this, but might tolerate it, if Peking were to have four other seats. The Republic of China would have to change its name. There would be bitter opposition to this scheme. In the long run, it might have to be chosen as an alternative to no seat at all for the Republic of China.

Communist Chinese membership in the United Nations is not a panacea. There will probably be no early alteration of Peking's behavior. Hostility to the United

States will probably become more intense. China's initial response will not determine the recommended action's soundness. The soundness must be judged on how well the action fits in with political realities; how much long-term influence there will be on the principals, and on third parties.

A Chinese proverb states that under Heaven all men are brothers. It augurs well for the future that the Chinese people have over the course of their long history shown themselves to be a practical people. They are likely to accept a balanced and workable solution to this Chinese puzzle as long as the solution is honorable. Lest Americans be too fearful, they should remember that good does often flow from what may at first seem to be a dangerous course of action. Americans strongly favor a large effective U. N. military force. Perhaps China may supply ample troops for such a force in future years. Would Communist Chinese troops, under U. N. command, have been evicted so fast by Nasser from the Gaza Strip?

Imagine the possibilities in Africa, if Chinese troops were to be transported to that continent in United States ships as part of a U. N. peace-keeping force. The view from South Africa would be different if Chinese troops were available on the African continent. Possibly, there might be a solution then to the problem of southwest Africa. A strong U. N. force could be highly persuasive. Russia might use its Security Council veto more responsibly if Peking had the veto, too. Admission of China to the United Nations would end an American policy begun in the Korean War. Before June, 1950, American foreign policy was based on the fundamental assumption that the Soviet Union presented the chief threat to American security. It still does. Like water under pressure, Soviet Imperialism goes where it is permitted to move. The main object of Moscow is still to fill every nook and cranny available to it in the basin of world power. When Russia finds barriers in its path which are unassailable, it accommodates itself to them, and looks for alternatives. We must never forget that the Russians will exert constant, increasing pressure toward the desired goal. The American task is still to erect "unassailable barriers" in the path of Soviet power in order to contain its further spread. The People's Republic of China as a member of the United Nations may assist America in that policy of containment. An unassailable barrier referred to here does not have to be an ABM System, nor additional missile-firing capability. It could just as well be an arms-race limitation treaty with proper inspection safeguards.

The United States must continue pro forma to oppose the admission of the People's Republic of China to the United Nations. To do otherwise would make the issue too big a matter in domestic politics. The China lobby in the United States can still make itself heard. When the Committee of One Million begins to act on these matters, the ghosts of McCarthyism can be called upon easily.

On 21 September, 1961, the Committee of One Million sponsored a rally in Carnegie Hall. Senator Dodd, the principal speaker, stated that the Committee of

One Million would lead a campaign to take the United States out of the United Nations, if Communist China won a seat. "If the United Nations goes over the precipice, I don't think anything can save it," Dodd said. "It shall by its own act," he continued, "forfeit the respect and confidence of honest men everywhere. It shall by its own will swallow the poison which shall destroy its heart and soul, and leave only an empty shell."[2] Many other members of Congress will sound a similar call, if the United States makes an abrupt change in its policy of opposition. American public opinion is not far enough advanced to permit a major shift in the United States for several years.

Peking does not want the United States to change its policy of opposition. Some Chinese delight in the exclusion. A victory, when it comes, will be sweeter yet, because it will be a defeat for the United States. A triumph for Peking, involving humiliation for the United States, might go a long way in satisfying hurt Chinese feelings.

The specific problem in the United States is to change public opinion before it is too late. There will be no effective nuclear nonproliferation treaty without China. China will sign no treaty until it is a recognized member of the international community with full rights in the United Nations. Chou En-lai speaking to the closing session of the National People's Congress on 10 April, 1960, stated categorically that no international agreement made without the participation of China would have any binding force whatsoever on China. China would not take part in a big-power conference, while the Chinese People's Republic was not recognized. A government which is not recognized could not go to a conference with those other governments which did not recognize it. Peking categorically refused to sign the Nuclear Test-Ban Treaty of 1963.[3]

The press in the United States has performed poorly in shaping public opinion. The press itself deplores what Arthur O. Sulzberger, president and publisher of the *New York Times*, described in a commencement address at Bard College, on 23 June, 1967, as a "dismaying, almost terrifying ignorance" about current affairs on the part of the public. Sulzberger said that the average man lives in a world that continually baffles him. It is difficult for him to hold a valid opinion about world problems. The man glances at a few headlines and goes about hoping for the best.[4] The reconciliation of democratic government, in which public opinion must be consulted, with the need for action on such a question as Chinese representation in the United Nations, is a key problem. It has been too easy for a demagogue to make a domestic political issue out of the China question. It is not an academic problem. Nuclear proliferation possibilities brought President Johnson and Premier Kosygin together at Glassboro. The possibility of a Chinese thermonuclear bomb in Egyptian hands is not now remote.

Walter Rathenau, the German Statesman, who negotiated the Treaty of Rapallo, gave instructions which could be usefully followed now. Rathenau was assassinated in 1923. Had he lived, it is possible that Hitler might never have come to power. It was Rathenau's idea that leadership should pass to those creative men who were not only intellectuals, but who were also men of action. The men with the strong, hard bodies, and the keen, open, liberal minds should take active steps to change American public opinion, so we will not look at China as a nation to be ignored and feared; but, rather, as a member of the international community to be respected and dealt with as a potential friend of America.

The point must be made to American society that democracy may be our system of government, but it is not necessarily the only, nor the best system of government for all peoples. Forms of Socialism may be better for some people; there is nothing intrinsically wrong with Socialism. As a social system, it is more noble than Capitalism. The essence of Capitalism is selfishness. That is an evil of the system with which we must live, because it gives, in return, great advantages; liberty, and the right to exercise our free will. Pure Communism is the system which is doomed to destruction, not Capitalism. Eventually, this will be recognized in China, as it has been in Russia. Communism considers man as we would like him to be, and not as he is. Therefore, it is not practical in the pure forms. Communism forgets in its theory that men are sometimes lazy, selfish, and corrupted by power. The capitalistic system is not particularly noble. The most affluent members of our society are not the captains of industry, but those who heal the sick. The advantage of our system, despite its many faults and inequalities, is that it works, and it provides for individual free choice.

There is no need for the enduring, unreasoning fear of Communism, or of the People's Republic of China. The enemy to be feared is Imperialism—everywhere—whether it be economic Imperialism, or Russian Imperialism. In dealing with the problem of Communism, we must attack it at the source, that is, use remedies which bring social justice, and thus help to eradicate the areas where Communism flourishes. We must never fear to negotiate, but we must negotiate from strength and knowledge, and not from fear and ignorance.

For years, Canada has led new thinking at the United Nations. If intellectual men of action like Dean Acheson, Averell Harriman, Senator Fulbright, Senator McGovern, McGeorge Bundy, and Roger Hilsman can change public opinion in the United States, Canada may eventually be able to take initiatives which will lead Peking into the United Nations, and which will be acceptable to the majority of the American people.

Unfortunately, Canada seems to be losing its heart for the job. Canada scolded the members of the U. N. in September of 1969. Secretary of State for External Affairs, Mitchell Sharp, told the General Assembly that too much attention to speeches and resolutions had permitted the budget to soar and the quality of work to drop.

The U. N. has been having trouble with a flood of paper and may even drown in a sea of words. Governments are beginning to attach less importance to U. N. activities. The credibility of the U. N. as a viable instrument for resolving the world's problems is wasting away.

In his criticism, Mr. Sharp recommended that U. N. members concentrate on top priority matters and generally adopt a more businesslike approach.

Finally, the Canadian diplomat urged U. N. members to develop a model for future peace-keeping operations. Past efforts in this area leave substantial room for improvement.

Aside from the problem of nuclear control, representation of the Chinese people in the United Nations is basically a matter of justice. Justice delayed is justice denied. The American people have a history of fellowship, magnaminity, and good will. Yet in America, justice has been denied to many citizens.

For almost two decades, the Chinese people have been internationally disenfranchised. The American people have been noble and fair, but on occasion, they have also been unjust. The Blacks in America were denied full citizenship for a century after the American Civil War. Almost twenty years after the Chinese Civil War, the people of China are still denied full international citizenship.

There is a philosophical basis, also, for Chinese representation in the United Nations. Pierre Teilhard de Chardin, in the *Future of Man*, seems prophetically apt in evaluating the present world crisis. He spent many years of his life studying the evolution of man in China. The great superiority over primitive man which we have acquired, and which will be enhanced by our descendants in a degree perhaps undreamed of by us, is in the realm of self-knowledge.[5] Our species is entering its phase of socialization. We cannot continue to exist without undergoing the transformation which, in one way or another, will forge our multiplicity into a whole. A whirlpool is beginning to appear ahead of us. The whirlpool is stronger than we are, but being men, we have the power of judgment to aid our navigation.[6]

Nothing exists or finally matters except the whole. For the elements of the world to become absorbed within themselves by separation from others, by isolation, is a fundamental error. The individual, if he is to fulfill and preserve himself, must strive to break down every kind of barrier which prevents separate beings from uniting. The exaltation of the individual is not egotistical autonomy, but of communion with others. Seen in this light, the modern totalitarian regimes, whatever their initial defects, are neither heresies, nor biological regressions: they are in line with the essential trend of "cosmic" movement.[7] If liberty is to be modified only and not lost, we must take steps to modify that "cosmic" movement of totalitarian regimes. No modification is possible without communication. The John K. Fairbank approach requires this communication. We cannot know our adversary unless we communicate with him. Maybe the People's Republic of China is not even our adversary. Perhaps communication with an imagined adversary will help us understand ourselves. There are none so blind as those who will not see. Men, and nations, too, at times, may be their own best friends. They are also, at times, their own worst enemies.

There is greatness and magnanimity in the American past. At Appomattox, Grant allowed the rebels to keep their horses for spring plowing. There are those who may think this to be a hackneyed story, yet it is nonetheless noble for being known to every schoolboy.

Grant did insist on the formal surrender of the infantry. General Joshua L. Chamberlain of the 20th Maine took the surrender. Chamberlain was an intellectual man of action. The former Bowdoin College professor was a modest man who had been severely wounded. He had the heart of a lion and greatness in his soul. Since Chamberlain had never been recognized for his gallantry, Grant asked him to take the surrender of Lee's army.

The leading division of the rebels was the old Stonewall Brigade, under the command of General Gordon, another superb soldier, and a man of ability and character. As Gordon passed Chamberlain, the Union Commander gave the order, and the entire first division of the Fifth Corps, Army of the Potomac, gave the marching salute to the rebels. Gordon caught the significance of the movement, and his whole attitude changed. He reciprocated the honor. Thus the two armies accorded each other the final recognition of two gallant opponents. The rebel soldiers went home to their farms, and did not go to the hills as guerrillas.

Now one century after Appomattox perhaps the United States can extend the magnanimous hand of Grant to China. Russia and China have not resolved their territorial disputes. Friendship between the United States and the People's Republic of China could be a stabilizing force in world politics and could lead us all down the road to *majesty, justice* and *peace.*[8]

FOOTNOTES

[1]Mao Tse-tung, *Quotations from Chairman Mao Tse-tung* (Peking: Foreign Languages Press, 1966) p. 216.

[2]Hilsman, Roger, *To Move A Nation* (New York: Doubleday & Company, Inc., 1967) p. 309.

[3]Tindel, Lyman M., Jr. (ed.) "The International Position of Communist China" *The Hammarskjöld Forums*, No. 5 (Dobbs Ferry: Oceana Publications, 1965) p. 31.

[4]*The New York Times*, 25 June, 1967, p. 70.

[5] Teilhard de Chardin, Pierre, *The Future of Man*, Translated from the French by Norman Denny (New York: Harper & Row, 1964) p. 16.

[6]*Ibid.*, p. 40.

[7]*Ibid.*, p. 46.

[8]Churchill, Winston, *Our Joint War Effort*.

APPENDIX A

A YEAR-BY-YEAR TABULATION OF THE UNITED NATIONS
GENERAL ASSEMBLY'S VOTES ON CHINESE REPRESENTATION.*

Year	For Nationalists	For Communists	Abstentions
1950	33	16	10
1951	37	11	4
1952	42	9	9
1953	44	10	2
1954	43	11	6
1955	42	12	6
1956	47	24	8
1957	47	27	7
1958	44	28	9
1959	44	29	9
1960	42	34	22
1961	48	36	20
1962	56	42	12
1963	57	41	16
1964	No vote held (assessment crisis)		
1965	47	47	20
1966	57	46	17
1967	58	45	17
1968	58	44	18
1969	56	48	21

The 1950 vote was on a proposal to seat Communist China. The votes from 1951 to 1960 were on proposals to shelve the question during the session. The votes from 1961 to 1969 were on proposals to seat Communist China and expel Nationalist China.

*Source: The Library of Congress, Legislative Reference Service

APPENDIX B

PUBLIC OPINION IN THE UNITED STATES ON THE QUESTION
"SHOULD COMMUNIST CHINA BE A MEMBER OF THE UNITED NATIONS?"*

Year	Should	Should Not	No Opinion
1950	11	58	31
1954	8	79	13
1955	10	67	23
1956	11	74	15
1957	13	70	17
1958	17	66	17
1961	18	65	17
1966	25	56	19

*Source: Gallup Political Index, Gallup-International

"DO YOU THINK COMMUNIST CHINA SHOULD OR SHOULD NOT BE ADMITTED AS A MEMBER OF THE UNITED NATIONS?"*

	October, 1966		
	Should	*Should Not*	*No Opinion*
	%	%	%
NATIONAL	25	56	19
Sex:			
Men	32	53	15
Women	19	58	23
Race:			
White	26	57	17
Non-White	x	x	x
Education:			
College	42	48	10
High School	25	59	16
Grade School	15	56	29
Occupation:			
Prof. & Bus.	35	51	14
White Collar	34	55	11
Farmers	18	58	24
Manual	20	60	20
Age:			
21-29 years	28	58	14
30-49	29	54	17
50 & over	21	56	23
Religion:			
Protestant	22	58	20
Catholic	27	54	19
Jewish	x	x	x
Politics:			
Republican	27	58	15
Democrat	23	57	20
Independent	28	50	22
Region:			
East	31	51	18
Midwest	24	58	18
South	17	57	26
West	31	58	11
Income:			
$7,000 & over	34	53	13
$5,000-$6,999	23	58	19
$3,000-$4,999	16	59	25
Under $3,000	15	58	27
Community Size:			
500,000 & over	33	50	17
50,000-499,999	21	62	17
2,500-49,999	29	54	17
Under 2,500	19	58	23

*Source: Gallup Political Index, October, 1966, p. 16.

APPENDIX C (2)

"SUPPOSE A MAJORITY OF THE MEMBERS OF THE UNITED NATIONS DECIDE TO ADMIT COMMUNIST CHINA TO THE UNITED NATIONS. DO YOU THINK THE UNITED STATES SHOULD GO ALONG WITH THE DECISION, OR NOT?"*

| | October, 1966 | | |
	Should	Should Not	No Opinion
	%	%	%
NATIONAL	53	33	14
Sex: Men	60	32	8
Women	47	34	19
Race: White	55	33	12
Non-White	x	x	x
Education:			
College	68	27	5
High School	53	36	11
Grade School	42	33	25
Occupation:			
Prof. & Bus.	66	25	9
White Collar	63	30	7
Farmers	41	41	18
Manual	47	38	15
Age:			
21-29 years	52	38	10
30-49 years	58	30	12
50 & over	49	34	17
Religion·			
Protestant	51	36	13
Catholic	55	29	16
Jewish	x	x	x
Politics:			
Republican	56	36	8
Democrat	48	34	18
Independent	61	29	10
Region:			
East	61	24	15
Midwest	54	35	11
South	36	44	19
West	62	30	8
Income:			
$7,000 & over	64	29	7
$5,000-$6,999	51	36	13
$3,000 $4,999	43	36	21
Under $3,000	37	39	24
Community Size:			
500,000 & over	59	26	14
50,000-499,999	53	36	11
2,500-49,999	51	37	12
Under 2,500	47	36	17

*Source: Gallup Political Index, October, 1966, p. 17.

APPENDIX C (3)

**"WOULD YOU FAVOR THE ADMISSION OF COMMUNIST CHINA
IF IT WOULD IMPROVE U.S.-COMMUNIST CHINA RELATIONS?"***

	Yes	*October, 1966* No	No Opinion
	%	%	%
NATIONAL	55	30	15
Sex: Men	60	30	10
Women	52	30	18
Race: White	57	30	13
Non-White	x	x	x
Education:			
College	67	27	6
High School	56	32	12
Grade School	45	30	25
Occupation:			
Prof. & Bus.	68	26	6
White Collar	59	31	10
Farmers	49	33	18
Manual	49	33	18
Age:			
21-29 years	65	24	11
30-49 years	58	29	13
50 & over	49	34	17
Religion:			
Protestant	53	32	15
Catholic	60	27	13
Jewish	x	x	x
Politics:			
Republican	53	34	13
Democrat	55	29	16
Independent	60	30	10
Region:			
East	63	23	14
Midwest	57	30	13
South	42	36	21
West	58	34	8
Income:			
$7,000 & over	64	28	8
$5,000-$6,999	54	32	14
$3,000-$4,999	47	29	24
Under $3,000	43	36	21
Community Size:			
500,000 & over	62	26	12
50,000-499,999	51	35	14
2,500-49,999	59	32	9
Under 2,500	50	31	19

*Source: Gallup Political Index, October, 1966, p. 18

BIBLIOGRAPHY

PUBLIC DOCUMENTS, United States

Public Papers of the Presidents of the United States: Harry S. Truman, Government Printing Office, 1950.

Public Papers of the Presidents of the United States: Dwight D. Eisenhower, Government Printing Office, 1961.

Public Papers of the Presidents of the United States: John F. Kennedy, Government Printing Office, 1963.

Public Papers of the Presidents of the United States: Lyndon B. Johnson, Government Printing Office, 1966.

United States Participation in the United Nations. Reports of the Presidents of the United States to the Congress, 1949-1965 inclusive.

Chinese Representation in the United Nations. The Library of Congress, Legislative Reference Service, Washington, D.C.: 1965.

China-USSR Boundary. International Boundary Study No. 64. Washington: Department of State, 1966.

Foreign Policy Briefs. U. S. Department of State.

American Foreign Policy 1950-1955. Two Volumes. Department of State. Washington: Government Printing Office, 1957.

Communist China, A Strategic Survey. Headquarters, Department of the Army, February, 1966.

Kennedy, John F. *Statements and Speeches Made During Service in the Senate and House.* Senate Document 79, 88th Congress, 2nd Session. Washington: U.S. Government Printing Office, 1964.

PUBLIC DOCUMENTS, U.N. and Foreign

United Nations Year Books
Official Records of the United Nations: General Assembly and Security Council.
U.N. Monthly Chronicle.
Department of External Affairs on Her Majesty's Service. Press Releases. Canada.
Norway in the United Nations.
The United Nations—Twenty Years of Failures and Success. Morozov and Pchelintsev. Moscow: Novosti Press Publishing House, 1965.
Britain and the United Nations. London: Central Office of Information, 1964.

BOOKS, Primary and Secondary Sources, U.S. and the West

Acheson, Dean. *Present at the Creation,* New York: W.W. Norton & Co., Inc., 1969.

Appleton, Sheldon. *The Eternal Triaangle? Communist China, The United States, and The United Nations.* Michigan State University Press, 1961.

Bloomfield, Lincoln F. *The United Nations and U.S. Foreign Policy.* Boston: Little Brown and Company, 1960.

——*The U.N. at Twenty and After.* Headline Series, No. 173. New York: Foreign Policy Association, 1965.

——. *International Military Forces.* Boston: Little, Brown and Company, 1964.
Brook, David. *The U.N. and The China Dilemma.* New York: Vantage Press, Inc., 1956.
Bundy, McGeorge, (ed.) *The Pattern of Responsibility.* Boston: Houghton Mifflin Company, Inc., 1952.
Burding, Andrew H. *Dulles on Diplomacy.* New York: D. Van Nostrand Company, 1965.
Burns, James MacGregor. *Roosevelt, The Lion and the Fox.* New York: Harcourt, Brace & World, Inc., 1956.
Chassin, Lionel Max. *The Communist Conquest of China.* Trans. T. Osato and L. Gelas. Cambridge: Harvard University Press, 1965.
Churchill, Winston S. *The Grand Alliance.* Boston: Houghton Mifflin Company, 1951.
——.*The Hinge of Fate.* Boston: Houghton Mifflin Company, 1951.
——.*Triumph and Tragedy.* Boston: Houghton Mifflin Company, 1953.
Claude, Inis L. *Swords into Plowshares.* Third Edition Revised. New York: Random House, 1964.
Dirland, Albert A. *The Chinese Puzzle.* Canadian Institute of International Affairs. Toronto: Baxter Publishing Co., 1966.
Doolin, Dennis J., *Territorial Claims in the Sino-Soviet Conflict.* Hoover Institution On War, Revolution and Peace. Studies: 7. Stanford University, 1965.
Doolin, Dennis J., and North, Robert C. *The Chinese People's Republic.* Hoover Institution on War, Revolution and Peace. Studies: 14. Stanford University, 1965.
Dmytryshyn, Basil. *A Concise History of USSR.* New York: Charles Scribner's Sons, 1965.
Eisenhower, Dwight D. *Memoirs.* 2 vols. New York: Doubleday & Co., 1963.
Fairbank, John K. *China: The People's Middle Kingdom and the U.S.A.* Cambridge: Belknap Press, Harvard University, 1967.
——. *The United States and China.* New York: Compass Books Edition, 1962.
Fitzgerald, C.P. *The Chinese View of Their Place in the World.* Chatham House Essays. Oxford University Press. London: Royal Institute of International Affairs, 1966.
Friedmann, W.W. *An Introduction to World Politics.* New York: St. Martin's Press, 1965.
Fulbright, William J. *The Arrogance of Power.* New York: Random House, Inc., 1966.
Gettleman, Marvin E. (ed.) *Viet Nam, History, Documents and Opinions on a Major World Crisis.* New York: Fawcett Publications, Inc., 1965.
Goodrich, L. Carrington. *A Short History of the Chinese People.* 3rd ed. The University Library, New York: Harper and Row, Publishers, 1959.
Grant, U.S. *Personal Memoirs of U.S. Grant.* 2 vols. New York: Charles L. Webster & Co., 1886.
Halperin, Morton H. *China and The Bomb.* Center for International Affairs, and The East Asian Research Center. Harvard University. New York: Frederick A. Praeger, 1966.
Hamm, Harry. *China: Empire of the 700 Million.* Trans. Victor Andersen. Garden City, New York: Doubleday & Company, Inc., 1966.

Hammarskjöld Forums. *The International Position of Communist China.* Fifth Hammarskjöld Forum. Lyman M. Tindel, Jr. (ed.). Dobbs Ferry, New York: Oceana Publications, Inc., 1965.

Herz, John H. *International Politics in the Atomic Age.* New York: Columbia University Press, 1962.

Hilsman, Roger. *To Move a Nation.* New York: Doubleday & Company, Inc., 1967.

Hull, Cordell. *The Memoirs of Cordell Hull.* 2 vols. New York: The MacMillan Company, 1948.

Hunt, Frazier. *The Untold Story of Douglas MacArthur.* New York: Signet Books, 1954.

Isaacs, Harold R. *Images of Asia, American Views of China and India.* New York: Capricorn Books, 1957.

Jackson, W.A. *Russo-Chinese Border Lands.* New York: D. Van Nostrand Company, Inc., 1962.

Kennan, George F. *American Diplomacy, 1900-1950.* Charles R. Walgreen Foundation Lectures. Chicago: University of Chicago Press, 1951.

Lederer, Ivo J. *Russian Foreign Policy.* New Haven: Yale University Press, 1962.

Lewis, John Wilson. *Communist China, Crisis and Change.* Headline Series, No. 179. New York: Foreign Policy Association, 1966.

Mendlovitz, Saul H. (ed.) *Legal and Political Problems of World Order.* Preliminary Edition. Boston: Spaulding-Moss Company, Inc., 1962.

Morison, Samuel Eliot. *The Maritime History of Massachusetts.* Sentry Edition. Boston: Houghton Mifflin Company, 1961.

Murphy, Robert. *Diplomat Among Warriors.* New York: Doubleday & Company, Inc., 1964.

Myrdal, Jan. *Report From a Chinese Village.* New York: Signet Books, 1966.

Niebuhr, Reinhold. *The Irony of American History.* New York: Charles Scribner's Sons, 1952.

Phillips, Cabell. *The Truman Presidency.* New York: The MacMillan Company, 1966.

Prezzolini, Giuseppe. *Machiavelli.* New York: Farrar, Straus and Giroux, 1966.

Reed, John. *Ten Days That Shook the World.* New York: Random House, Inc., 1960.

Schlesinger, Arthur M., Jr. *A Thousand Days.* Boston: Houghton Mifflin Company, 1965.

Snow, Edgar. *The Other Side of the River: Red China Today.* New York: Random House, 1961.

Sorensen, Theodore C. *Kennedy.* New York: Harper & Row, 1965.

Spanier, John. *American Foreign Policy Since World War II.* New York: Frederick A. Praeger, 1965.

———.*The Truman-MacArthur Controversy and the Korean War.* Published by arrangement with the Harvard University Press. New York: W.W. Morton & Company, Inc. 1965.

Tang, Peter S.H. *Communist China Today.* Vol. 1, 2nd ed., rev. and enl. Washington, D.C.: Research Institute on the Sino-Soviet Bloc, 1961.

———. *Russian and Soviet Policy in Manchuria and Outer Mongolia, 1911-1930.* Introd. Philip E. Mosely. Durham, N.C.: Duke University Press, 1959.

Teilhard de Chardin, Pierre. *The Future of Man.* Trans. Norman Denny. New
York: Harper & Row, 1964.
Throp, Willard L. *The United States and the Far East.* The American Assembly.
Columbia University. Englewood Cliffs, N.J.: Prentice-Hall, Inc., 1962.
Truman, Harry S. *Memoirs.* 2 vols. New York: Doubleday & Co., 1956.
Wanamaker, Temple. *American Foreign Policy Today.* New York: Bantam Books,
1964.
Ward, Barbara. *Spaceship Earth.* New York: Columbia University Press, 1966.
Whiting, Allen S. *China Crosses the Yalu.* The Rand Corporation. New York: The
MacMillan Company, 1960.

BOOKS, People's Republic of China

*People of the World Unite for the Complete, Thorough, Total and Resolute
Prohibition and Destruction of Nuclear Weapons.*
Ling, Soong Ching. *The Struggle for New China.* Peking: Foreign Language Press,
1953.
Vice-Premier Chen Yi Answers Questions Put By Foreign Correspondents. Peking:
Foreign Language Press, 1966.
The Kennedy Administration Unmasked. Peking: Foreign Language Press, 1962.
*Support the Just Stand of the Soviet Union and Oppose U.S. Imperialism's Uniting
of the Four-Power Conference of Government Heads.* Peking: Foreign Language
Press, 1960.
Oppose U.S. Military Provocations in the Taiwan Straits Area. A selection of
important documents. Peking: Foreign Language Press, 1958.
Oppose U.S. Occupation of Taiwan and "Two Chinas" Plot. A selection of
important documents. Peking: Foreign Language Press, 1958.
Kennedy and U.S. Imperialism. A Commentator's Article on Ahahata. Peking:
Foreign Language Press, 1964.
Oppose the New U.S. Plots to Create "Two Chinas." Peking: Foreign Language
Press, 1962.
Drive U.S. Imperialism Out of Asia. Peking: Foreign Language Press, 1960.
Quotations from Chairman Mao Tse-tung. Peking: Foreign Language Press, 1966.

NEWSPAPERS

Christian Science Monitor
International Herald-Tribune, Paris
Izvestia
New York Times
People's Daily
Pravda
Toronto Globe & Mail
Wall Street Journal
Washington Post

PERIODICALS

Australian Journal of Politics and History
China Quarterly
Current Digest of the Soviet Press
Global Digest
Harvard Journal of Asiatic Studies
Journal of Asian Studies
Peking Review
Problems of Communism
Swiss Review of World Affairs

PAMPHLETS

Behind the Headlines. The Chinese Puzzle. Canadian Institute of International Affairs. Vol. XXV, No. 6, August, 1966.
Human Rights, The Dignity of Man. Oceana-United Nations Study-Guide Series.
Reprints from the Soviet Press. Vol. III, No. 6, 13 October, 1966. New York: Compass Publications, Inc.
Studies on the Soviet Union. Siberia and the Far East. New Series, Vol. 5, No. 4, 1965. Institute for the Study of the USSR. Munich, Germany.
Synopses of United Nations Cases. Carnegie Endowment for Peace.
The World Must Eat, Problems of Food and Population. Oceana-United Nations Study-Guide Series.
The Trojan Horse of Neocolonialism. (U.S. Policy of Training Specialists for Developing Countries). Nikolai Yermolov Progress Publishers, Moscow.
United Nations Association of the United States of America. *China, The United Nations and United States Policy.* New York: 1966.
United Nations Work for Human Rights. United Nations, New York.

STATEMENTS of Government policy and copies of official speeches given out by various delegations to the United Nations. Given to writer in person by Agents of the delegation in the New York Offices of the Missions to the United Nations. Specific reference made in footnotes.

MISCELLANEOUS

Contemporary Archives and Statistics
Keesing's Contemporary Archives
Facts on File
Gallup Political Index
The World Almanac and Book of Facts

INDEX